FabJob®

FabJob Guide to

Become an Etiquette Consultant

Lori Benjamin and Mary Snyder

**FABJOB® GUIDE TO
BECOME AN ETIQUETTE CONSULTANT
by Lori Benjamin and Mary Snyder**

ISBN-13: 978-1-894638-35-7
ISBN 10: 1-894638-35-2

Library and Archives Canada Cataloguing in Publication

Benjamin, Lori
FabJob Guide to become an etiquette consultant /
by Lori Benjamin and Mary Snyder.

Accompanied by CD-ROM.
Includes bibliographical references.
ISBN-13: 978-1-894638-35-7
ISBN-10: 1-894638-35-2

1. Etiquette consultants. 2. New business enterprises.
I. Snyder, Mary, 1963- II. Title. III. Title: Become an etiquette consultant.

HF5389.G62 2005 395.023 C2006-903058-8

About the Websites Mentioned in this Guide: Although we aim to provide the information you need within the guide, we have also included a number of websites because readers have told us they appreciate knowing about sources of additional information. (**TIP:** Don't include a period at the end of a web address when you type it into your browser.) Due to the constant development of the Internet, websites can change. Any websites mentioned in this guide are included for the convenience of readers only. We are not responsible for the content of any sites except FabJob.com.

FabJob Inc.
19 Horizon View Court
Calgary, Alberta, Canada T3Z 3M5

FabJob Inc.
4603 NE University Village #224
Seattle, Washington, USA 98105

To order books in bulk, phone 403-949-2039
To arrange an author interview, phone 403-949-4980

www.FabJob.com

About the Authors

Lori Benjamin is the Director of World Class Etiquette Ltd.®, where she develops and presents a full range of programs in business and social etiquette, international protocol and cultural awareness. She has also been an instructor of etiquette programs for children and adults through the University of Calgary, and she designs and delivers etiquette programs for the local Board of Education. She also gives etiquette and protocol presentations to many corporations and professional associations, and offers corporate and social etiquette consultations.

Business

Downtown returns tomorrow

World-class act

As an author of *Mind Your Manners*, a weekly etiquette column for the Sun newspaper chain, Lori was interviewed as an etiquette expert by dozens of media outlets throughout North America. She has also been featured giving etiquette advice in two television series, including the nationally televised *Men's Style*. Mrs. Benjamin has been active in many community organizations, including the Chamber of Commerce, Better Business Bureau, and Executive Women International. She has judged several beauty pageants, and been involved with a wide variety of charitable organizations.

Mary Snyder is a freelance financial and business writer, a small business owner, and the executive director of a non-profit organication, Etc. Mary formerly worked as a regional sales and marketing manager for a human resources company, where her company excelled at matching people with careers. This combination of skills gives Mary a unique ability to write about career choices such as the one in this book. As the co-author of a financial how-to book, Mary's work has been featured in national, regional, and local publications. Her comments have appeared in a wide variety of newspapers, magazines, newsletters, and websites including *The Washington Times*, MSN.com, CNN Money, *Parent Guide Magazine* (New York), *Working Woman, Mademoiselle*, and *Parenting*.

Acknowledgments

The authors and editors would like to thank *Susan Geist* for editorial assistance.

Thank you to the following etiquette experts, listed alphabetically, for generously sharing career advice and information on etiquette consulting:

- *Pamela Bedour*
  Founder and director of The Protocol School of Ontario
  www.psoo.com

- *Millie Chastain*
  Etiquette consultant and founder of The Protocol School of Alabama
  www.protocolschoolofalabama.com

- *Phyllis Davis*
  President of Executive Mentoring and Coaching International and author of *E^2 – Using the Power of Ethics and Etiquette in American Business*
  www.mycoach.com

- *Melba S. Lim*
  Etiquette consultant and former diplomat
  Pomona, California

- *Dorothea Johnson*
  Founder and director of the Protocol School of Washington and Board of Directors member of the International Association of Protocol Consultants®
  www.psow.com

- *Mary Mitchell*
  Etiquette expert and author of *The Complete Idiot's Guide to Business Etiquette*
  www.themitchell.org

- *Michele O'Reilly*
  Director of The Connecticut School of Etiquette, LLC
  www.morethanmanners.com

- *Colleen Rickenbacher*
  Etiquette specialist and author of *Be on Your Best Business Behavior*
  www.colleenrickenbacher.com

- *Jodi R.R. Smith*
  President of Mannersmith Etiquette Consulting in Boston
  www.mannersmith.com

- *Tish Spaulding*
  Director of Spaulding Protocol in Birmingham, Alabama

- *Gloria Starr*
  Founder of Global Success Strategies, Inc., Toronto, Chicago, San Francisco, North Carolina and Palm Beach
  www.gloriastarr.com

- *Jacqueline Whitmore*
  Author of *Business Class: Etiquette Essentials for Success at Work* and director of The Protocol School of Palm Beach
  www.etiquetteexpert.com

Contents

1. Introduction

Congratulations! You have just taken the first step on the path to a dream career as an Etiquette Consultant. Your love for good manners and social graces can soon become the basis of an exciting and lucrative new career.

You will discover how to get started and succeed in this fabulous career in this guide, the *FabJob Guide to Become an Etiquette Consultant*. In this chapter, you will read about the importance of etiquette in people's lives, see why there is increasing demand for professional etiquette consultants, learn about the many benefits of this career, and discover the steps to take to get started.

1.1 Welcome to Etiquette Consulting

If you ask five people what *etiquette* means, you will likely get five different answers ranging from knowing which fork to use, to when to send a thank-you note. Many people consider etiquette to be something you use when you're at a fancy dinner or meeting dignitaries, but etiquette is more than just knowing how to navigate a place setting or how to introduce your business partner.

According to Princeton University's *Wordnet*, etiquette can be defined as: "rules governing socially acceptable behavior." The online encyclopedia *Wikipedia* recently described the norms and effects of etiquette as follows:

> "Etiquette fundamentally prescribes and restricts the ways in which people interact with each other, and show their respect for other people by conforming to the norms of society. Modern Western etiquette instructs us to: greet friends and acquaintances with warmth and respect, refrain from insults and prying curiosity, offer hospitality equally and generously to our guests, wear clothing suited to the occasion, contribute to conversations without dominating them, offer a chair or a helping arm to those who need assistance, eat neatly and quietly, avoid disturbing others with loud music or unnecessary noise, follow the established rules of a club or legislature upon becoming a member, arrive promptly when expected, comfort the bereaved, and respond to invitations promptly."

"Etiquette is all about behavior," says Jodi R.R. Smith, president of Mannersmith Etiquette Consulting in Boston and a professional etiquette consultant with more than 17 years of experience. "It's about knowing the right behaviors so you are comfortable in all situations and you make other people comfortable."

1.1.1 The Importance of Etiquette

If you have ever sat across the table from someone with bad table manners, overheard someone speaking loudly on their cell phone, or had your questions to a customer service representative answered with "yeah," "I dunno," or "whatever," then you understand why etiquette matters.

As *Wikipedia* notes, "Violations of etiquette, if severe, can cause public disgrace, and in private hurt individual feelings, create misunderstandings or real grief and pain, and can even escalate into murderous rage."

People make quick judgments based on the way someone talks or behaves, and these impressions can be tough or even impossible to change later. However, people aren't always aware of the impressions they are making, or they are not sure how to act in certain situations. That's when your services as an etiquette consultant can make a difference. With your help, the sloppy eater who offended those around him can be transformed into the charming gentleman who everyone wants to invite to dinner.

An understanding of etiquette can help people make the right impression the first time. As an etiquette consultant you will offer guidance to people who need to conduct themselves with poise. You will teach people manners and give them with the skills they need to be confident in themselves and their conduct.

You'll have the chance to work with a wide variety of people and impact their careers and their lives. You may teach business professionals everything from how to handle a soup spoon to how to run an international sales meeting. You'll share your love of good manners with children and their parents in seminars and workshops. You can teach international protocol to up-and-coming politicians and other people of power, so they can interact successfully in a multicultural setting.

As an etiquette consultant you will provide people with essential skills they need to succeed in business and in life. You will have the chance to work with a wide variety of people. You will help them win admirers, get contracts, and earn promotions, because they will be one of those people who always knows the right thing to say or do... courtesy of you!

1.1.2 The Etiquette Industry

Etiquette is sometimes believed to have arisen from ceremonies developed at the court of King Louis XIV of France in the 17th century. However, etiquette has been important in all civilized societies, from the time of ancient Egypt, through the days of ancient Greece and Rome. In ancient China, Confucius is reported to have included rules for speaking and eating with his philosophical teachings.

Today etiquette consulting is in demand from the corporate arena to the school classroom. As a professional etiquette consultant you will be joining a booming industry. A 2002 *New York Times* article reported that etiquette training programs are increasing in popularity and cited several reasons, including:

- The global economy's demands on executives to be sensitive to foreign cultures;
- The decline in human interaction in the high-tech workplace; and
- The social ineptitude of younger managers who grew up in households where proper manners were not encouraged.

As the economy tightens, businesses are seeking ways to be more competitive in the market, and many find training their employees in the basics of etiquette can pay off in the long run. When a business takes the time to train employees on the intricacies of foreign protocol, foreign clients notice and respond. When employees know how to handle themselves in any situation, clients notice and feel that their business will be handled with the same correctness.

Since *The New York Times* article was written, the etiquette industry has continued to grow. Jacqueline Whitmore, founder and director of The Protocol School of Palm Beach, reported in April 2005 that her business had actually tripled since September, 2001 — a period of about three-and-a-half years.

Millie Chastain, a certified etiquette consultant in Alabama, began her career after retiring from the Georgia school system. She opened the Protocol School of Alabama in Talladega, Alabama, and after only two years in business, the school was thriving. "I never realized there was such a huge need for this business," said Chastain.

Dorothea Johnson, founder and director of the Protocol School of Washington, has seen a huge increase in the demand for her services. There is a long waiting list to attend a training course at the Protocol School of Washington. Many of these potential trainees are employed by companies that are looking to add etiquette training to the list of services they offer to employees.

While some companies hire etiquette consultants on contract, other companies hire someone to handle the etiquette training for the company full time. As an etiquette consultant you can be self-employed or work in a variety of industries. For example, you could work for a recruiting firm, training job candidates about business etiquette and helping them prepare for executive-level interviews. Or you could work with the hospitality industry, training staff on international protocol, etiquette basics, and communication skills.

In addition to working with businesses, you might be hired by parents to teach etiquette skills to children, work with colleges and universities to groom soon-to-be graduates, or oversee protocol for international events. You could even decide to use your skills in a governmental setting such as working with an embassy.

1.1.3 Etiquette Categories

Etiquette consultants provide services in a variety of areas which can be divided into different categories as described below.

> **TIP:** Etiquette categories often overlap and you can combine categories to suit your clients' specific needs. For example, you may have a client who needs to know business dining etiquette or business communication etiquette.

Business Etiquette

Business etiquette, also known as corporate etiquette, covers how people behave in business settings. As an etiquette consultant you might offer specific training in one area of business such as telephone etiquette, or you might cover a variety of situations including: business meetings, introductions, business cards, handshakes, email, corporate gift giving, business dining, and doing business overseas.

Children's Etiquette

Also known as etiquette for young people, this category involves teaching etiquette to children ranging from pre-schoolers to high school seniors. Etiquette consultants will normally hold classes for specific age groups, such as age 3-5, 6-12, and 13-16.

Topics might include addressing adults, introducing friends, table manners, thank-you notes, talking on the telephone, and other aspects of social etiquette for children.

Communication Etiquette

Communication etiquette covers many of the areas listed above under business etiquette. However, it may encompass communication in social settings as well as in business. If you choose to specialize in this area, you may teach people about conversation skills, telephone etiquette, email etiquette, thank-you notes, making introductions, and other aspects of interpersonal communication.

Dining Etiquette

Which fork goes with the salad and why do I have so many spoons? Which glass is for water and which one is for wine? These are just a few of the questions that you'll hear from clients regarding dining etiquette. This type of training is often done "hands-on" in a dining environment, so clients can learn by doing. Private dining etiquette consultations are highly requested, according to many etiquette consultants.

International Protocol

International protocol, also known as international etiquette, covers how to interact with people from foreign countries. According to *Wordnet*, protocol means "forms of ceremony and etiquette observed by diplomats and heads of state." However, protocol is used by all kinds of people doing business overseas or hosting a guest from another country. If you decide to teach international protocol, you may cover status and forms of address, proper attire, making introductions, effective gift giving, dining customs, and other aspects of doing business or interacting with people from other cultures.

Social Etiquette

Social etiquette involves etiquette in social situations. Many etiquette consultants who offer social etiquette focus on social gatherings, such as dinners and parties. Topics may include being a good host, being a polite guest, making toasts, and invitations. It is often combined with dining etiquette.

Wedding Etiquette

While the rules of social etiquette apply to weddings as well as other social occasions, etiquette consultants are often asked for advice about issues specifically related to weddings. Examples include: who pays for what, who to invite, who sits where, whether it's okay to ask for cash gifts, who hosts the shower, etc.

1.1.4 Benefits of an Etiquette Consulting Career

There are many reasons why etiquette consulting is an excellent career choice. The benefits of a career as an etiquette consultant include:

Financial Success

As you will read later in this book, etiquette consultants can earn high hourly and daily fees for their services. As an etiquette consultant employed full-time by an organization, you can earn a salary comparable to other professionals. If you start your own etiquette consulting business you could earn $100,000 or more per year. Business etiquette expert Phyllis Davis told us she charges $500 per hour for one-on-one consultation, and $10,000 per day for corporate training and workshops.

Rewarding Work

Of course being an etiquette consultant isn't just about the money, it's about sharing your love of good manners and social graces with adults and children, and it's about offering your services to help people succeed in business and in life. You'll be working with all types of people, at all stages of life. You might be coaching a shy teenager one day and training a class of executives the next. You can go to bed at night feeling like you made a difference in people's lives that day. And if you keep in touch with your clients, you can follow their successes as they move through life, knowing you had a hand in making them who they are.

Opportunity to Learn

If you love to learn, etiquette consulting is an ideal career. Most etiquette consultants have a library full of reference books and enjoy giving advice about a wide range of topics. While much of the advice remains constant, this field is constantly evolving.

A few decades ago, there was no such thing as "email etiquette" or "cell phone etiquette." As an etiquette consultant, you can keep on top of new developments and be the expert people turn to when they aren't sure what to do.

Freedom

If you start up your own etiquette consulting business as many of the experts quoted in this guide have, you will have the more obvious benefits of being self-employed: tax write-offs, setting your own hours, and spending less time commuting and more time with your family.

You Can Start Right Now

Unlike other occupations that can cost thousands of dollars and require years of education, you can become an etiquette consultant no matter what your current situation is. No degree is required to become an etiquette consultant, and you can start your own etiquette consulting business at home with few upfront expenses. If you have access to transportation, a computer, and a phone – you have what you need to get started.

1.2 Inside This Guide

The *FabJob Guide to Become an Etiquette Consultant* will take you step-by-step through getting started and succeeding as an etiquette consultant. These steps, and the chapters they appear in, are as follows:

Chapter 2 (*Preparing for Your Career*) describes the skills clients and employers are looking for in etiquette consultants. In this chapter you will discover how to learn etiquette consulting through educational programs, mentoring, volunteering, and self-study. This chapter lists a variety of programs you can take to become certified as a professional etiquette consultant. You will also learn about jobs that can prepare you for a career in etiquette consulting, and discover how to create your own full-time job as an etiquette consultant.

Chapter 3 (*How to Do Etiquette Consulting*) explains different types of consulting, including one-on-one coaching and presenting etiquette training for groups. You will learn how to offer these services, including how to meet with clients and evaluate their etiquette needs, how to develop a plan of action, and how to present training programs. This chapter includes many helpful samples you can use in your own etiquette consulting business, including client questionnaires, and an overview of key areas of etiquette that you can advise clients about.

Chapter 4 (*Starting Your Own Business*) gives practical information on what you need to do to start an etiquette consulting business, including how to set up your office, choose a business name, and set your fees. The chapter also covers small business basics and includes helpful forms such as a sample contract and sample invoice you can adapt for your own business.

Chapter 5 (*Getting Clients*) will teach you how to find clients for your business. This chapter explains how to market your business with a variety of techniques including advertising and publicity. You will also learn how to approach corporate clients and put together a proposal that wins you their business.

Chapter 6 (*Success Stories*) offers stories from people who have been where you are, have achieved success in their careers as etiquette consultants, and who offer personal advice and guidance. The guide concludes with a list of helpful Resources for learning more about etiquette.

Inside the *FabJob Guide to Become an Etiquette Consultant* you will find a wealth of information to help you on your way to becoming a professional etiquette consultant. In addition to the insight and expertise of the authors, this guide incorporates advice from some of the most respected and well-known etiquette consultants in North America. They have been where you are, and are extending a professional hand to help you become an etiquette consultant.

When you are finished with this guide you will know what steps to take next and where to go from there. By applying what you learn here, it's just a matter of time before you'll be where you want to be — in a rewarding career as an Etiquette Consultant.

2. Preparing for Your Career

While some careers require many years of formal education, you may already be prepared to enter a career in etiquette consulting. If you are well-mannered, knowledgeable about etiquette, and skilled at communicating with people, you have a solid foundation for success in this career.

In this chapter you will discover specific skills needed by etiquette consultants, and learn how to prepare for a career in etiquette consulting by developing those skills. The chapter explains how to learn through self-study as well as professional etiquette consultant training programs.

2.1 Your Manners

Perhaps the most important "skill" for an etiquette consultant to have is impeccable manners. Once people learn your profession, they will pay attention to how you talk, make introductions, or even eat a meal. (Of course, many of the people you meet will be more concerned about the impression they are making on you.)

Like a celebrity who can't go out – even to the supermarket – without always looking fabulous, people will notice if you ever display any behavior they perceive as not good etiquette. If you are always well-mannered, this won't be a concern. However, there may be times when you are tired, hungry, upset, or simply in a hurry. Can you be "on" even at those times?

Chances are you already have excellent manners, or you would not be considering a career in etiquette consulting. However, it may help to have a refresher of some of the social situations where others will notice your manners.

2.1.1 Dining Etiquette

When you take a seat at a formal dinner, you may find yourself face-to-face with a jumble of silverware, glassware, and china. First, let's identify everything that you will see in a place setting, we'll then look at what happens during a formal meal, and discuss how to handle dining mishaps.

Place Settings

Deciphering the map of the table can help you ease into formal or informal dining situations. To eliminate the confusion of which plate to use or which glass is yours, remember this rule of thumb: Anything to do with food is located on your left and anything involved with beverages is found on the right.

The bread plate, then, is to the left of the dinner plate, whereas the wine glasses are to the right. The napkin is placed either on the dinner plate or tucked to the left of the plate. Examples of both informal and formal place settings appear on the next page. Note that you may have more or less silverware or glassware, depending on the establishment and the meal being served.

You also will likely have individual salt and pepper shakers, a place card, and a menu card. A place card will have your name printed on it and the menu card will have the upcoming meal courses printed on it.

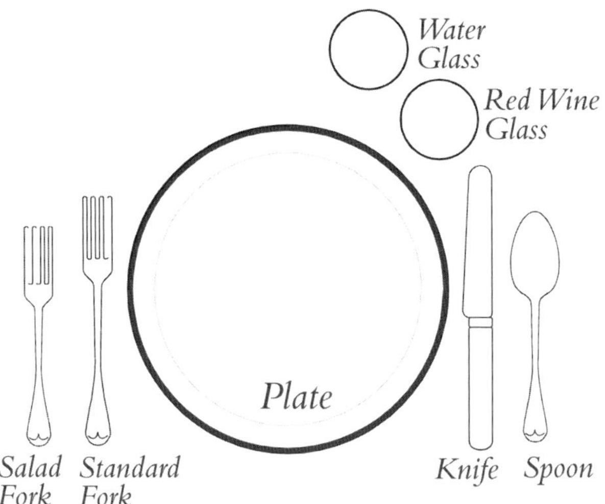

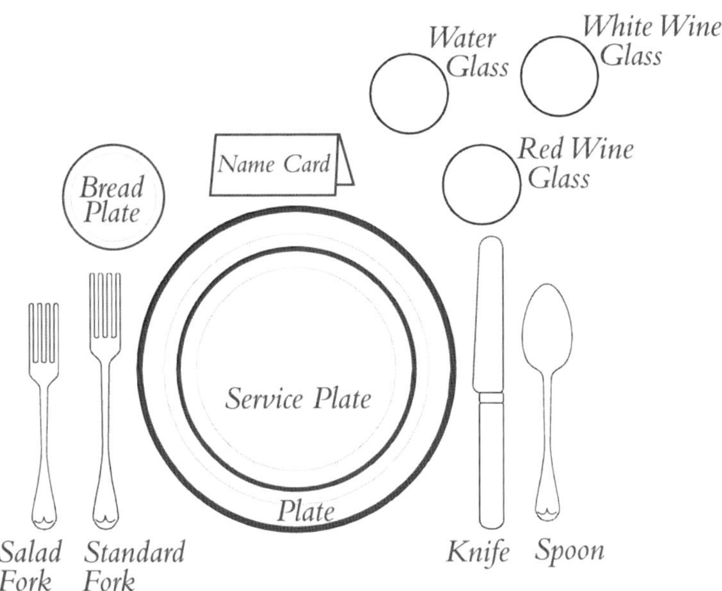

Plates and Bowls

The place plate is the main dinner plate. If soup or salad, or both, are served, they will come to the table in the bowl or plate and later be removed. The salad plate is served on top of your dinner plate and the soup bowl is served on a service plate that sits on top of your dinner plate. The plates are often sitting on a charger plate, which is an oversized plate for your place plate to sit on.

There may also be a small bowl and a small plate above your place plate. The bowl is your finger bowl for cleaning your hands and the plate is for dessert. Sometimes these are served to you after the meal, but there are occasions when these are placed on the table ahead of time.

Silverware

In a formal place setting you will have a host of silverware. Starting from the outside left and going across, there are the:

- Seafood fork
- Salad fork
- Dinner fork

Then (closest to the plate on the right, and moving away from the plate), the:

- Salad knife
- Dinner knife
- Seafood knife
- Soup spoon
- Cocktail fork (which is often placed with the tines resting in the soup spoon)

Above and to the left of the dinner plate (just above the forks) is the bread and butter plate, and lying across the plate is the butter spreader (or butter knife). Directly above the dinner plate is the dessert fork (with tines facing right), and dessert spoon (aimed left).

As mentioned, not all utensils will be at every table depending on the establishment and the meal served. However, even at a more casual affair you will find the forks to the left of your plate and the knives and spoons to the right. An easy rule to remember is that you work from the outside of the setting inward.

> **TIP:** Any silverware not used may be left in place. Once you use your silverware it should never touch the table again.

Glassware

In a formal setting you will have five glasses. These are positioned to the right of your place plate and above your knives. Again, you will usually work from the outside in. The glasses, from the farthest right, are:

- **Sherry or aperitif glass:** served with the soup
- **White wine glass:** usually served with the fish
- **Red wine glass:** usually a wider, larger glass to allow the wine to breathe
- **Water glass:** usually just above the dinner knife; the largest glass on the table
- **Champagne flute:** located behind the water glass; usually used with dessert

Styles of Eating

There are two acceptable ways to use your silverware — American and Continental (or European).

The people of the United States and Canada use the American style of eating. The knife is held in the right hand with the index finger no more than one inch down the blade. The fork is held in the left hand with the tines pointed down. After the food is cut, you lay the knife near the top of the plate with the cutting edge facing into the plate and switch the fork to you right hand. You may either pick the food up with the fork tines or by sliding the tines underneath the food.

When you've finished your meal, you place your knife and fork, with the tines up, on the plate with the handles at the four o'clock position. This tells the waiter to remove your plate.

In the Continental or European style of eating, you hold the silverware the same way as in the American style; you just don't switch the fork to the right hand to eat. Using your left hand you place the food in your mouth. You will use the same position on your plate to indicate you are finished with your meal, except you will place your fork tines down.

> **TIP:** Don't wave your silverware as you make your point in the conversation. If you must use your hands to discuss a topic, then lay your silverware down on your plate.

The Dining Experience

Your formal dining experience will involve several courses and several wines (remember that moderation is always best!). Be aware of the pace of the meal. You don't want everyone waiting on you to finish before moving on with the next course.

Place your napkin in your lap, and use it throughout your meal. Just dab your lips and fingers as needed. Don't use your napkin to wipe down your silverware (ask for another set of cutlery if necessary).

Also, don't place your elbows, sunglasses, keys, purse, or cell phone on the table. In fact, cell phones and pagers should be set to "vibrate" or turned off at the table so they are neither seen nor heard.

Particularly if you are in a restaurant that specializes in an international cuisine, it's fine to ask the waiter for suggestions. You may want to say something like: "I enjoy chicken, what would you suggest I try?"

Posture is as important at the table as it is at any other place. Sit up straight with your back several inches from the chair. Elbows should be kept away from the tabletop until the meal is over and all dishes have been cleared. Even then, you should not lean heavily on them. During the meal, you can rest your wrists on the edge of the table. In Europe, it is considered poor table manners to place your hands in your lap during a meal — hands should always be above the table.

If you would like something from the table, it is polite to ask for it to be handed down. Never reach across the table to pick it up. If you need to leave the table, you should excuse yourself and place your napkin on your chair.

Bread

Bread will be placed on the table, passed around the table or placed in an individual container above your bread plate. If the breadbasket is in front of you, pass the basket to your right without taking a piece and when the basket comes around to you, remove your piece of bread. If you would like butter for your bread, take a pat of butter and place it on your bread plate. Do not butter your bread directly from the butter dish. Use your butter spreader, which is placed across your bread plate. Butter one bite of bread at a time, not the whole piece of bread.

Soup

Soup is often the first course in a formal meal. The soup may be hot or cold and it may be served in a bowl or in a cup. A clear soup is served with a large oval soup spoon and a cream soup is served with a small round soup spoon.

Soup can be a tricky appetizer to eat gracefully. The trick is to dip the spoon into the soup and scoop away from your body. When the spoon is about two-thirds full, sip the soup from the side of the spoon. Avoid putting the entire spoon in your mouth, sipping from the front of the spoon, or slurping the soup. It is acceptable to tip the bowl slightly to make it easier to spoon the last bit of soup from the bottom of the bowl.

You should not, however, lift the bowl off the table or sip from the bowl. If your soup is too hot, don't blow it, just stir the soup and spoon from the outer edges of the bowl. Once you have finished your soup, place your spoon on the plate under the bowl. Never leave your spoon adrift in the bowl.

Salad

A salad may be served before or after the main entrée. Here's a hint: where your salad fork is placed can tell you when to expect the salad. If your salad fork is placed to the left of the dinner fork, then you can expect the salad first. If the fork is placed to the right, then expect the salad to follow the main course. You will also likely have a salad knife at your setting, which is smaller than the dinner knife. You can use it to cut lettuce into manageable pieces.

Sorbet

Sorbet is often served to cleanse the palette between courses. You only need to have a taste or two; it is not necessary to finish off the dish.

Main Entrée

The main course is usually beef, chicken, duck, or lamb. You use your dinner fork and dinner knife to eat these dishes. Once you have finished your meal, place your silverware on your plate with the handles pointed to the four o'clock position (tines face down or up as is your preference) to indicate you have finished the meal. Don't push your plate or bowl away when you are finished, or use a toothpick at the table.

Finger Bowls

A finger bowl may be presented to you after the main course is complete. This small bowl is filled with warm water and a slice of lemon. Dip your fingertips in the bowl and dry them with your napkin. Place the bowl to the left of you and the waiter will take it away.

Dessert

Dessert will be served at the end of a meal. This may be cake or ice cream. You should have both a dessert spoon and a dessert fork. Use the spoon for the ice cream and the fork for the cake.

Handling Dining Accidents

It happens to everyone: the dropped fork or spilled wine. What is the best way to handle these dining mishaps? Here are a few of the most common dining accidents and suggestions on how best to handle them.

- If you drop your fork or spoon, discreetly ask the waiter to provide you with another. Don't worry about fishing around under the table for the wayward silverware, the wait staff will see that it is retrieved. If you are in a private home, lean down and retrieve the utensil and, again, discreetly request replacement.

- If you knock over a glass of wine or water, allow the waiter to clean up the spill and get on with the meal. If the spill happens in a private home, just dab up what you can with your napkin and your host should step in to help with the spill. Apologize and then get on with the meal.

- If your meat is undercooked, don't eat it. This is a potentially dangerous situation. Call your waiter over and discreetly explain the situation. They will most likely remove your plate and replace it with another properly cooked meal. The key here is discretion. There is no need to call attention to the situation.

- If you find yourself with a mouthful of gristle or a piece of a bone, you can discretely remove the item with the tines of your fork. Place this article under a piece of garnish or another portion of food. You don't want a chewed-up piece of gristle on display for everyone to view.

Foods That Are Meant to Be Eaten by Hand

- artichokes
- asparagus (if not covered in sauce or cooked until quite soft)
- crispy bacon
- bread
- cookies
- corn on the cob
- fried chicken
- french fries
- hamburgers
- canapés
- hors d'oeuvres
- sandwiches
- berries on the stem and small fruits

When you are ordering from a menu, remember to stick with foods that are easy to manage. You don't want to be wrestling with a lobster and trying to talk business at the same time. The same goes for messy foods. Barbecue ribs may be the specialty of the house, but unless you want to spend half your evening concerned that your face is covered in sauce, skip the ribs. If you do come face-to-face with a messy or awkward meal, here are some coping strategies:

- **Spaghetti:** It's difficult to twirl the spaghetti just so. If you are faced with this dish, use your fork and your spoon. Just grab (with your fork) a few strands of spaghetti, place the fork tines in your spoon and spin. Once the strands are tightly wound around your fork, you can eat it. Just remember to keep those bites small.

- **Barbecue ribs:** Use your fork and knife to trim off tiny bites. Not the best way to eat barbecue, but the cleanest way!

- **Lobster and crab:** These dishes are served with bibs, and you'll need yours. A shell cracker tool will also be served with these. Using your shell crackers and cocktail forks, you should be able to manage your way through cracking the shells and pulling out the meat. If you aren't sure how to start, just watch how the others are doing it or ask the waiter for instructions.

- **Sushi:** This Japanese favorite is served in bite-sized pieces. You can eat this with chopsticks or a fork, or with your hands if a hot towel is provided first. You lightly dip your sushi in a small bowl of soy sauce and wasabi, and eat the sushi in one bite. The pickled ginger is served to refresh your palette in between bites of sushi, so eat only a small amount. Try to eat everything you have ordered, as leaving food is an insult to the sushi chef.

Don'ts of Dining

Gloria Starr of Global Success Strategies offers the following additional dining don'ts:

- Don't put liquid in your mouth while you are still chewing
- Don't chew with your mouth open
- Don't talk with food in your mouth
- Don't mash your food together on a plate
- Don't tuck your napkin into your clothing
- Don't fiddle with cutlery or you'll appear nervous
- Don't leave the spoon in your coffee cup or lick it after stirring
- Don't lean back on the legs of your chair
- Don't reapply cosmetics at the table

2.1.2 Hosting a Dinner Party

As the host of a dinner party, you will have a list of things to attend to. Below is a sample checklist you can use as a guide to hosting a dinner party.

Sample Dinner Party Hosting Timeline

6 to 8 Weeks Before the Event

- ❑ Determine a date and a location for your event (plan earlier if your location is difficult to book).

- ❑ Decide if you will have the party in a restaurant, a private dining room or in your home. If you do have a dinner party at your home you may decide to have it catered or you may make the meal yourself.
- ❑ Create a guest list.
- ❑ Decide on the menu or work with the caterer or restaurant chef for meal options.

3 to 4 Weeks Before the Event

- ❑ Send out invitations with date, time and type of event (formal, semi-formal, etc.), and directions.
- ❑ Book the entertainment.
- ❑ Buy or rent any additional supplies you may need (trays, platters, chairs, tables, etc.)
- ❑ If you are hosting the dinner in your home, set aside time to purchase centerpieces, to set up your home for the dinner party, and to purchase and prepare the food.

One Week Before the Event

- ❑ Follow up with any guests who haven't responded.
- ❑ Make out seating arrangements.
- ❑ Make arrangements for parking.
- ❑ Plan your table décor.

The Night of the Event

- ❑ Welcome each guest as they arrive. If this is a restaurant or private dining room at a hotel or restaurant, position yourself at the entrance and greet each guest individually.
- ❑ Offer each guest a drink. Have both alcoholic and non-alcoholic on hand.
- ❑ Make certain that you have place cards for each person or show them to their seat personally. Invite the dinner guests to be seated.

- ❑ Introduce guests to one another.
- ❑ Offer the toast to guests and, if applicable, to the guest of honor.
- ❑ Say goodbye to guests as they leave and thank them for coming.

The host should pace their meal so they don't finish eating before the last person at the table. None of their guests should eat alone. If you are the host, and you offer more food to your guests, avoid asking if they would like 'another' serving. This suggests that they have already eaten enough. Instead, offer additional helpings in the same manner that you did the first time around.

If a guest asks for the salt, place both the salt and pepper shakers on the table in front of them. They should not be handed from guest to guest, and other guests should not intercept the shakers and use them. They should be passed to the original guest first. While this may not be the most efficient method, it is the polite one.

The host will often take the responsibility of filling wine glasses as well. These glasses should be filled only half full. At times, other guests will take on this role. If serving yourself wine, you should always refill the rest of the glasses first before filling your own.

Being a Polite Guest

Here are some tips to help you be a polite guest at a dinner party:

- Respond to an invitation within a day or two of receiving it.
- Do not be late, but also, don't arrive too early. Your hosts may not be ready for you. Try to arrive very close to the event start time.
- When the host invites dinner guests to be seated, sit only when everyone is beside their chairs. Guests sit from their left (and the chair's right) to avoid collisions when taking their seats.
- Make small talk with other guests. Whether this is before you are seated or after, make it a point to get involved in a conversation. (See section 2.1.4 for conversation tips.)
- Use dining etiquette as described earlier in this chapter.

- Leave at the end of the event. If there is no appointed end time, take your cue from the hosts and the other guests. Usually an hour after dinner ends is a good time.
- Say thank you to your host before you leave and send a thank-you note within a couple of days of the event.

2.1.3 Making Toasts

You can make a toast with wine, champagne or just mineral water. It isn't the drink that matters but the sentiment you are presenting. Here are a few toasting tips:

- Make sure that your toast is appropriate for the gathering and the guests.
- Be prepared. Take time to write and rehearse your toast. However, don't read the toast, do it from memory.
- End your toast with a positive note. "Cheers" always works well.

International Toasts

European and Asian countries have a strong tradition of toasting. In many foreign countries, the host of the meal will start off with a toast of welcome. It's a good idea to learn the local equivalent of "Cheers!"

Language	What to Say
Chinese	Wen Lie!
French	A votre sante!
German	Prosit!
Greek	Yasas!
Hebrew	L'Chayim!
Irish	Slainte!
Italian	Alla Salute!
Japanese	Kanpai!
Spanish	Salud!

- Be brief. Keep your sentiment to just a few short sentences. A sample business toast might be: "To Mr. Harris, whose leadership has made it possible for Acme Industries to be such a great success. Cheers."

While toasting doesn't have the hard rules of other dining etiquette, there are some accepted guidelines at special events. Christening toasts are offered at the luncheon following the christening or a luncheon to honor the christening. Godparents offer the first toast to the child; parents offer the second toast; siblings and any guests offer the rest. You can find tips on wedding toasts in section 3.4.5.

2.1.4 Conversation

Being a good conversationalist can draw people to you and enhance your overall image. As a professional etiquette consultant, you can demonstrate your good manners through every interaction. Everyone you encounter, from janitor to company president, should be treated with the same graciousness. Here are some tips for specific aspects of conversation.

Introductions

The purpose behind conversation is to form and build upon relationships. It can be intimidating to enter a room and not know anyone, but there are easy rules to follow when it comes to initiating social interaction with someone you don't know.

- First, approach the person with a smile on your face. This friendly gesture puts people at ease and shows that you want to connect with them.

- Be sure to make eye contact as you approach someone. Eye contact helps establish a connection and rapport between people.

- When entering a room full of strangers, find a person or group of people who look receptive to newcomers. People who stand with body language that appears open to the rest of the room (e.g. arms uncrossed, body not directly facing someone else) and who often look around the room are great targets for conversation. Finding a person or group of people who are carrying on a light and friendly conversation can make the transition easier.

- Always offer your name and ask for the other people's names.

Names

It's key to remember the other person's name. One way to do this is to use the name immediately in conversation. If you happen to miss the name during an introduction or can't recall it, come clean and ask the other person to repeat it.

To avoid awkward encounters, always present your name when you run into people you've met only a few times before. This refreshes the other party's memory, ensures they know your name, and allows them to concentrate on the conversation rather than searching their mind for who you are. Adding where you met them so they can put your face into context is a good idea as well.

Introductions tell you what a person wants to be called. Respect that. If a person introduces himself as "Michael" or herself as "Rebecca," use the full form of the name. Wait until you are invited to call him "Mike" or her "Becky." After all, if your new friend wanted to be called Mike or Becky, they would have introduced themselves as such.

Some names, especially foreign ones, can be difficult to pronounce. Take the time to learn how to properly say someone's name. This shows that you care enough to put forth an effort.

Making Small Talk

Conversation at cocktail parties, business seminars, the bus stop, and baby showers all follows the same basic principles. It may be called small talk, but it can be larger than life. You don't have to be extroverted and experienced to master the art of small talk. All you need is some simple instructions and practice.

Conversation is like a tennis match — you receive the ball, swing at it, and send it back over the net. The hope is that other people will then add something of their own and send the ball back to you. When the ball is in your court, provide some information and then turn it over to your conversation partner. By being warm and engaging, other people can easily add their experiences to the conversation. Conversation is two-sided, and both parties should feel comfortable sharing ideas and anecdotes.

A unique piece of jewelry or article of clothing can spark a discussion. Jewelry and clothing can also indicate a person's affiliations and hobbies — for instance, a person wearing a lapel pin may be advertising their membership in the Rotary Club. A team or business logo on a shirt or hat can tip you off to a person's occupation or sports loyalty. Don't let these opportunities pass you by. Use your powers of observation to make conversation easier.

It's important to let a conversation evolve and flow naturally. If a conversation is going well, do not change the subject. Once a topic is spent, ease into another subject to boost the energy level and recharge the conversation.

What Not to Say

The old adage remains true today: when it comes to conversation, don't talk about religion and politics. These days, those aren't the only taboo subjects to avoid in conversations. Some topics can bring a conversation to a screeching halt. Here are some areas that are best avoided when getting to know new people:

- Avoid passing on rumors or gossip.
- Don't tell questionable stories or jokes.
- Do not dwell on personal misfortunes, especially those that are current.
- Discussion about the costs of items can be uncomfortable.
- Don't ask how much a person earns or discuss your own salary.
- Don't delve into your health problems and concerns or the other person's health (unless the other person is suffering from something obvious and temporary, such as a cast).
- Avoid discussing controversial subjects (including religion and politics), especially when you don't know where the other person stands on them. If these topics do come up, try to take a neutral stance when you are with clients, business associates, or people you do not know well, even if you hold strong opinions on the subject.

- It is best to avoid talk about negative items in the news (for example, divorce or bankruptcy), as you don't know what the other person is experiencing or has gone through in the past.

Listening

Good conversationalists are good listeners. You should not only listen well but also show that you are listening. Lean toward the speaker to express your interest in what they are saying.

A key to listening and absorbing what you hear is repeating in your head what the other person is saying. Then paraphrase (restate in your own words) what was said to confirm your understanding.

Keeping eye contact and facing the speaker can also help you become a better listener. Ask questions if you missed something that was said — the act of questioning forces you to process the information. These tips help you show proper respect to the other person in your conversation and encourage the sharing of ideas.

What to Say About Rudeness

What does an etiquette consultant do when people behave rudely? In some situations, the answer is obvious. For example, if your child is rude you can correct his or her behavior. However, when you are dealing with people who are not your offspring or clients, what to do may be less clear.

For example, how should you handle it if you give someone a gift and don't receive a thank-you note, or you hold a party and you have to call people who haven't RSVPed to let you know whether or not they will attend?

When faced with rudeness, an etiquette consultant should generally take the high road, respond graciously and avoid giving the rude person a "free sample" of etiquette consulting by correcting their behavior. You can make a significant impact on people by your own polite behavior and you will likely find those who want etiquette guidance will ask for your advice.

2.1.5 Telephone Etiquette

Your conversation skills should extend to the telephone as well, especially because etiquette consultants are often asked to train people on telephone etiquette. The following gives you some guidelines and some sample scripts to work with.

Making a Call

When you make a call, the first thing you should do when someone answers the phone is identify yourself and then make your request. For example: “Hello, this is John Smith. May I speak with Susan Jones, please?” Once you have your person on the line, it is polite to ask if this is a good time to talk. If it is not a good time, then ask when would be the best time to call back.

Answering a Call

In this day of voicemail technology, answering your phone indicates that you are available to talk. If this isn't the case, then politely explain that this isn't a good time and ask if you can return the call. And then return the call. If you have an assistant who takes your calls, or if a spouse or child answers your calls, make certain that they ask the caller to leave a message and a number.

Call Waiting

Call waiting is a "beep" during a phone conversation to let you know someone else is trying to call, and it can be tricky to handle politely. When the phone beeps, should you immediately ask the other party to hold while you check to see who is calling? And what if you check and then you go back to your original caller and tell them that you must talk to this latest caller? Does that say to Caller Number One that Caller Number Two is more important?

The most polite option is to stay with your first conversation, if possible. If you must take the second call, do so, then quickly explain to Caller Number Two that you are on the other line and offer to call them back as soon as you complete your conversation with Caller Number One.

If the second call mandates your attention right away, be polite with Caller Number One and offer a valid explanation for taking the call. For example: "Jane, I am so sorry but that is my son on the line and he missed his flight to Denver. May I call you back as soon as I handle this?" This lets Caller Number One know that they are important, but an emergency has come up that requires your attention.

Caller I.D.

Caller I.D. is a display on your phone of who is calling (or beeping through), who called while you were out, and when the call came in. Caller I.D. was created to help you screen telemarketers and stop harassing phone calls, and can also be useful to help you prioritize your calls (for example, staying with a business call when your sister is trying to get through for her weekly chat).

When you use caller I.D. to screen your callers, don't answer your phone with "Hi, Bob!" even if you know it is Bob calling. Continue to use the traditional "Hello." When you return calls of friends who have called you while you were out, let them know you saw their number on your caller I.D. so they know why you are calling.

It is impolite to call numbers that you aren't familiar with just because they appeared on your caller I.D.. Maybe it was just a wrong number.

Answering Machines and Voicemail

A majority of people and businesses use voicemail or an answering machine to take calls when they're away from the phone or too busy to answer. Virtually everyone is comfortable with this technology, but there are still a few pointers to keep in mind. First, you should make an effort to listen to and respond to messages in a timely manner, preferably within one business day.

Your Outgoing Message

This is the message your machine or service will play when you are unavailable. Keep it brief and to the point. As you can advise your clients, no one wants to hear all three minutes of your favorite song, or a message that may be inappropriate for children. Make sure that your outgoing message includes the following:

- Your name
- Company name (if applicable)
- Request for the caller's name, message, and phone number
- Commitment to return the call

Here is a sample outgoing personal message:

> "Hello, you've reached the Smith residence. We're unable to come to the phone, but your call is important to us. Please leave your name, number and a message. We'll get back to you as soon as possible."

Here is a sample outgoing business message:

> "Hello, you've reached Etta Klette, with Etta's Etiquette. I'm away from my desk, but please leave your name, number and a message and I'll return your call. Thank you for calling."

Leaving a Message for Others

Sometimes it seems unlikely that you'll ever speak with a person when you navigate a series of automated messages telling you to "press one" or "press two", which will just take you to another series of "press one" or "press two"s. While this maze of messages is frustrating, don't let your frustration become apparent when you do finally talk to a real live person. The message you leave for others should include the following:

- Your name
- Company name (if applicable)
- Your brief message
- Your phone number

TIP: Don't leave a message with upsetting news. Request the person return your call.

Here is a sample business message:

> "Hello Mr. Smith, this is Etta Klette with Etta's Etiquette and I'm calling to follow up on the proposal I sent to you last week. Would you please call me at 555-1234? Thank you."

Here is a sample personal message:

> "Hi Sam. This is Etta. I was calling to see if you would like to have lunch next week. Does Thursday work for you? Please call me when you get a chance. My number is 555-1234."

Speaker Phones

Speaker phones were once only found in offices, but some people enjoy having one in their home. The main thing to remember with a speaker phone is that you must let the caller know that you are using a speaker phone, and that other people may be with you. You don't want the caller to say something inappropriate before realizing that this isn't a private conversation.

Cell Phones

More than a decade ago cell phones were a rarity, but today cell phone conversations are everywhere.

Jacqueline Whitmore, founder and director of The Protocol School of Palm Beach and the cellular phone etiquette spokesperson for Sprint, offers these tips:

- Let your voicemail take your calls when you're in meetings, courtrooms, restaurants or other busy areas. If you must speak to the caller, excuse yourself and find a secluded area.

- Speak in your regular conversational tone and don't display anger during a public call. Speaking loudly or showing emotion may distract those around you.

- If you are expecting a call that can't be postponed, alert your companions ahead of time and excuse yourself when the call comes in. The people you are with should take precedence over calls you want to make or receive.

- When walking and talking on your wireless phone, be aware of your surroundings and remember to respect the rights of others.

- Use your vibrate function or turn off your phone in public places such as movie theaters, religious services, and restaurants. Many wireless phones now have environmental settings that automatically adjust the phone and its features so you do not disrupt your surroundings.

- Practice wireless responsibility while you are driving. Place calls when your vehicle is not moving. Don't make or answer calls while in heavy traffic or in hazardous driving conditions. Use a hands-free device in order to help focus attention on safety. And always make safety your most important call.

- Use discretion when discussing private matters or certain business topics in front of others. You never know who is within hearing range.

2.1.6 Thank-You Notes

Sending thank-you notes is an important part of good manners. While many people know that a thank-you note is expected after a job interview, it is also expected in the following situations:

- When you receive a gift
- When you've attended a party
- When you've been a guest in someone's home
- Whenever someone goes out of their way to do something kind

Although email has made communication much easier these days, thank-you notes should ideally be handwritten and delivered within a few days of the event. Your thank-you note can be brief, but it should be specific. For example, rather than saying "thanks for the gift" it should say what gift you are thankful for.

Sample Thank-You Note

Dear Jan and Chris,

What a fun dinner party! I had a wonderful time and the steak was fabulous. It was great to meet Ms. Maison. Thank you so much for including me.

Warm regards,

Polly Proper

2.2 Developing Your Skills

While excellent manners are a prerequisite for this career, there are a number of other skills you will need. If you ask professional etiquette consultants what it takes to succeed in this career, you may hear a variety of answers. Jacqueline Whitmore, founder and director of The Protocol School of Palm Beach, offers this summary of the factors she feels lead to success in etiquette consulting:

> "You must have the managerial and business skills of a corporate executive; the charm and energy of a salesperson; the sensitivity and wisdom of a diplomat; and the discipline and focus of an athlete."

While many of these skills can certainly help you in any career, there are several skills that are particularly useful for etiquette consultants to have, including:

- Research skills
- Communication skills
- Business skills

2.2.1 Research Skills

Unless you already know everything there is to know about etiquette, there will be times you will need to "look it up." In fact, one of the advantages of working in this career is that you don't need to have a memory that holds as much information as an encyclopedia.

While clients will certainly expect you to have basic knowledge of etiquette, and you'll quickly learn answers to the questions you are most frequently asked, it is acceptable to let people know you will need to check with your sources to ensure your client receives the most up-to-date information. This is particularly important in a field such as international protocol, where accepted behaviors can vary tremendously from one country to another, and may change over time or with a new government.

Although you don't need to know everything about etiquette before you become an etiquette consultant, it is essential that you have access to etiquette information, and know how to find the answers.

Most of your information is likely to come from printed materials or online research. If you take an etiquette certification program (see section 2.3.1), you will likely receive printed information about the area of etiquette you have studied. But whether or not you attend an etiquette training program, you will very likely find the following to be valuable resources:

Books

Many etiquette consultants have a library of etiquette reference books they can turn to. If you check Amazon.com, you will find hundreds of etiquette reference books offering advice on everything from what to say in a thank-you note to how to handle a foreign dignitary.

Chances are you already have at least a few books in your home library, and once you start an etiquette consulting business any reference books you purchase should be tax-deductible (check with your accountant to be certain).

Your local public library can also be a good source of information because etiquette is a consistently popular topic so most public libraries have a wide selection of books. However, while a public library can be useful for tracking down classic etiquette books, more recent information can sometimes be difficult to come by, as popular books may be checked out when you go to look for them.

To assist you in selecting books, the Resources chapter of this guide lists dozens of etiquette books in different categories (children's etiquette, dining etiquette, business etiquette, etc.)

Online Resources

If you found this guide on the Internet, chances are you are already a skilled online researcher and know how to quickly find etiquette information online. If you are fairly new to the Internet, the editors of this guide suggest the following tips for conducting online research:

- Start with the Google search engine at **www.google.com**. While any search engine will give you some results when you search for information about etiquette, Google's sophisticated technology often gives more relevant results than a search engine such as Yahoo.

- Be specific with your searches. If you do a search for a general term such as dining etiquette, you will find there are hundreds of thousands of web pages, and you may have to read through a lot of information that isn't relevant before finding what you're looking for. If you search instead for the specific information you want, such as "using a finger bowl", you are much more likely to find the answer you want on the first page of the search results.

TIP: Include quotation marks before and after the phrase you're searching for to get results that contain the exact phrase you want to find.

- Verify the information. It is wise to confirm any information you find on the Internet, even if you trust the source. By checking more than one source, you may find more current information or discover regional differences in what is considered proper etiquette. For example, in some places it is considered rude not to remove shoes when entering someone's home, while in other places removing footwear at the door might be considered odd behavior.

In addition to the helpful free information available online, the Internet is also a source of excellent reference material that you can purchase inexpensively. For example, if you have a client that needs information about doing business overseas, as you will see in section 3.4.3 of this guide, you can purchase up-to-date reports about different countries at prices ranging from $4 to $24 per country.

2.2.2 Speaking Skills

Working as an etiquette consultant requires being able to speak with people beyond your own circle of friends and associates. Chances are you will be working with a mix of people who you may never have worked with before. You may find yourself making a presentation to a group of third graders, their teachers and parents one day, then coaching the president of a Fortune 500 company the next day.

And you will be doing a lot of speaking. You will speak about your programs when you sell your services to decision-makers. You will speak about etiquette to clients either one-on-one or in a group setting. You will speak to civic and professional groups about the need for etiquette skills.

So you will need to develop skills that allow you to speak effectively both interpersonally (one-on-one) and in front of groups of people.

Interpersonal Communications

Consultants with excellent interpersonal communication skills speak clearly but they also listen well. You need to hear what your clients are saying to you and often you must go beyond the words to find the meaning.

For example, Suzy Smith wants you to teach her how to manage a formal dinner. This is a simple consultation, but during your initial interview you learn she's just been hired by a company that hosts formal dinners for clients from many countries. By listening to your client you can suggest some additional consultation in international protocol along with the formal dining training. Not only are you gaining more business, you are also looking out for the best interest of your client.

> **TIP:** Having excellent interpersonal communication skills starts with having good manners, so make sure you read the previous section, particularly the parts about conversation and listening.

While good manners are essential, as a professional consultant, you will be expected to offer more than charming conversation. It is easy to talk about how lovely someone's home is, or how delightful their party was. It is not so easy to tell someone they must correct their behavior.

In a career that addresses what is wrong with a person's behavior, it's important to communicate in a way that avoids having clients feel attacked or invalidated. Rather than being "brutally honest" with people, etiquette consultants communicate honestly but diplomatically. Make sure that you offer people positive feedback, as well as telling them what needs to be corrected. Your clients have to like you, trust you and believe you have their best interest in mind when doing business with you.

On the next page you will find examples of "words that help" and "words that hurt" when communicating with people during a presentation. The same principal applies when communicating one-on-one. Your choice of words, tone of voice, and body language can communicate disapproval or they can communicate that you are there to help.

Words that Help

Any of the following (and expressions like them) can help to create a positive learning environment.

- Thank you for sharing that
- You're right
- That's a good point
- I see what you mean
- That's an interesting idea

Words That Hurt

Just as there are words that can encourage participation, any of the following (or expressions like them) can discourage participation:

- You're wrong
- Are you kidding?
- That's ridiculous
- Where did you ever get that idea?
- That's not true

It is also best to avoid terms like "always" or "never" (as in, "you must always ..." or "you should never...") because absolutes can lead to arguments. When you must disagree with someone, follow the guidelines in section 3.3.8.

If this is an area you want to improve, a fabulous resource used by many professionals is the book *How to Win Friends and Influence People,* by Dale Carnegie.

Presentation Skills

Speaking to a group can be more challenging than speaking with an individual because the group may include people with a variety of preconceived ideas about etiquette. There may be audience members who feel that etiquette is (a) something they already know all about; (b) something only Grandma cares about; and/or (c) boring. It will be your job to make etiquette an engaging, relevant topic for your audience.

As an etiquette consultant you will of course be expected to provide excellent information about etiquette. Your speech or workshop should always give your audience something of value they can take away with them. It might be as simple as learning which fork to use for salad, or it may be the knowledge that international protocol is essential to succeed in a global economy.

However, if you plan to present information about etiquette to groups, you need to provide more than good information. Tag Goulet, author of the *FabJob Guide to Become a Motivational Speaker*, explains why:

> For the past 10 years I have been teaching public speaking to adult students at university. At the end of every semester, each student gives a speech and is evaluated by classmates. Some of the students do a tremendous amount of research for their speeches. Others focus less on the research and more on their delivery. Over the years the students have been consistent in their evaluation. They have a clear preference when it comes to which types of speakers they prefer. So, who do you think rates higher?
>
> (a) A speaker with fabulous information and so-so delivery
>
> (b) A speaker with fabulous delivery and so-so information
>
> The answer is (b). Of course, the ideal situation is to have both fabulous information and fabulous delivery. However, for many audiences, your delivery is the most critical factor and it can make a significant difference in how the information is perceived. **Poor delivery can make the most interesting topic sound boring, while excellent delivery can make even a dull topic come alive.**

Here are four traits Tag has identified that can help you deliver your information about etiquette in a way that will be well received by audiences:

- **Confident:** Professional speakers may sometimes feel nervous, but they don't let it show. (And they don't tell the audience they feel nervous!) Confidence is often judged on the basis of non-verbal factors. Speakers look and sound more confident when they make eye contact with the audience, move naturally, use audiovisual equipment effectively, and speak fluently (avoiding too many "uhs" and "ums").

- **Credible:** Credibility is an audience's perception of how believable or trustworthy a speaker is. To be credible, a speaker must be seen as someone who is both an expert on the topic and a likeable person.

- **Dynamic:** Dynamic speakers are enthusiastic about their topic, and they share that enthusiasm with their audience through variety and energy in their voice, gestures, and body movements. Other terms that can be applied to these speakers are "high energy" and "passionate."

- **Natural.** Natural speakers don't lecture. Even when speaking in front of an audience of thousands, they speak as if they were having a conversation with a group of friends. Other terms that may be applied to these speakers are "real" or "down-to-earth."

There are a number of ways to enhance the traits described above, and improve your presentation skills:

Practice Public Speaking

As with any skill, one of the best ways to improve is by just doing it. With speaking, this means getting yourself in front of as many audiences as possible. One excellent way to do this is by volunteering to present talks on etiquette to community groups. This is covered in detail in section 5.3.2. You can also get practice in speaking by taking a continuing education course. Many colleges offer courses in public speaking, from intensive two-day seminars to courses held several hours a week over an entire semester. Check the Yellow Pages for local colleges and universities. If you can't find a listing for continuing education, call the school's main switchboard.

Sample Speaker Evaluation Form

Speaker's Name: ______________________________

Title of Speech: ______________________________

Date: ______________________________

Please rate the speaker's performance in the following areas on a scale of 1 (poor) to 5 (excellent).

Delivery:	**Poor**				**Excellent**
Rate of speech (too fast or slow, just right)	1	2	3	4	5
Volume/audibility (too loud, too quiet)	1	2	3	4	5
Enthusiasm	1	2	3	4	5
Eye contact with audience	1	2	3	4	5
Appropriate gestures/facial expressions	1	2	3	4	5
Personal connection made with audience	1	2	3	4	5
Content:					
Clear central idea	1	2	3	4	5
Speech contained useful information	1	2	3	4	5
Speech was free of irrelevant information	1	2	3	4	5
Speaker avoided using technical terms	1	2	3	4	5
Organization:					
Introduction created interest in the topic	1	2	3	4	5
Speech was logical; easy to follow	1	2	3	4	5
Main idea(s) were clearly communicated	1	2	3	4	5
Sufficient information to support main points	1	2	3	4	5
Visual aids were used effectively	1	2	3	4	5

General Comments:

1. What did you find most useful about this program? Least useful?

2. What else would you like to see included in this program?

3. What was your overall impression of the speaker?

Another way to improve your skills is to join Toastmasters, an international non-profit organization that helps people develop speaking skills. Toastmasters clubs usually meet for an hour per week, and provide the opportunity to practice speaking. The cost to join is $20, plus dues of $27 every six months ($21 dollars if your local club is outside of the Toastmasters district). Local Toastmasters clubs may also charge small fees to cover their expenses. To find a chapter near you, check the phone book, visit the Toastmasters website at **www.toastmasters.org** or call their headquarters at (949) 858-8255.

Ask for and Use Feedback

While simply getting practice speaking in front of audiences can help you become a more confident speaker, you can also use these occasions as an opportunity to get feedback.

An easy way for audience members to give you feedback is by filling out evaluation forms. On the facing page is an example of a speaker evaluation form that you can give to your audience to get feedback and ratings in a number of different areas. (Of course you can ask about specific areas you want feedback on.) You will get more honest feedback if the people filling out the forms remain anonymous.

The following websites offer good advice to help with your presentations:

- *3M Meeting Network – Delivering Presentations*
  www.3m.com/meetingnetwork/presentations/delivering.html

- *Epson Presenters Online*
  www.presentersonline.com/basics/delivery

- *117 Ideas for Better Business Presentations*
  http://117ideas.com

- *Presentations with Punch*
  www.members.shaw.ca/toasted/new_page_2.htm

2.2.3 Business Skills

If you are interested in starting your own etiquette consulting business, you will find it easier if you have basic business skills. In Chapter 5 you will find detailed advice on two skills essential for business success –

how to market your business and sell to clients, so we won't repeat that information here. Instead, this section focuses on organization skills that will help you in the day-to-day running of your business.

Organization

Being a successful etiquette consultant means keeping up with training materials, client files, bills, and all the paperwork that a successful business generates. You may choose to use file cabinets and paper files for each client, or you may decide to go with something a bit more high tech and keep all your client information in a computer database.

Keeping Track of People

Contact management systems help you keep track of all the little bits and pieces of information that you'll want to have at your fingertips, and business cards you want to keep. Let's say you spend the afternoon at a Chamber of Commerce luncheon and meet several people. Anne Smith is interested in communications etiquette for her staff, and she asks you to call her in two weeks to set up an appointment. Joe Green wants to talk to you next week about one-on-one training for his teenage daughter. And Sammy Howard is interested in learning more about Chinese protocol.

You note all this information on the backs of each person's business card; then with contact management software, you can log it into your system. The software lets you set up and maintain very extensive contact logs. It also has calendar and appointment logs, phone dialing capabilities, and alarms that notify you when to follow up with your contacts. Examples of contact management software include ACT! and Microsoft Outlook. Chapter 4 has advice on how to find software for your business.

Keeping Track of Information

Your office will be filled with all sorts of reference materials, from books to magazine articles on etiquette. And if you are doing any international etiquette training, you'll have material on different countries and regions of the world.

Newsletters and individual pages of materials can be kept together in a three-ring binder. Magazines can be kept together in magazine files:

little cubbies for multiple magazines, which fit great on bookshelves. Books can be stored on shelves in closets, cabinets or on bookshelves. Computer disks can be stored in boxes that are made specifically for this use, just make sure to label your disks so you can easily find your research material.

Keeping Track of Your Schedule

As an etiquette consultant, you also have to learn how to organize your day and your schedule. This may sound easy, but that isn't always the case. Some people struggle to be organized. Other people tend to over-schedule themselves and then can't meet their obligations.

Consider using a hand-held PDA (Personal Digital Assistant) or a planning system such as *Franklin Planner*, *Day-Timer* or *Day Runner* to keep on track. You can find planning systems at any office supplies store. Having a planning system will help you keep your day on target, but you have to know how to use it, and use it regularly to make it work effectively.

Create a list of things to complete each day — this is your "to do" list. This list can include meetings, phone calls to make, and even just time

to relax and regroup. But it's not enough just to have a list. Time management requires you to prioritize your schedule. You have to decide what the most important tasks are on your list, and get those done first. Set up a time every day, as early as you can handle, or even the night before, to write and prioritize your list.

Give each item in your list a letter designation, A or B. A must be completed today and B would be good to complete today, but can be completed tomorrow. Once you've decided what has to be done and what can be put off for a day, then rank your tasks in the order of importance.

Try to note the amount of time it will take to complete a task, even though some will be easier to judge than others. You can set aside one hour to practice your latest training presentation, but you don't always know how long a new client meeting will run. Try to make a good estimate. If you usually spend an hour and a half with new clients, then schedule for an hour and a half, but be prepared if the meeting runs longer. See Chapter 4 for a variety of resources and more ideas to help you successfully run an etiquette consulting business.

2.3 Ways to Learn Etiquette Consulting

The good news is you don't need years of education and training to become an etiquette consultant. However, investing some time and possibly some money into extra training can set you on a path for success. So let's take a look at some different ways you can learn the business of etiquette consulting.

2.3.1 Certification and Education

Although you do not need a certificate to become an etiquette consultant, you may learn more efficiently and effectively by taking an educational program that leads to a certificate. Professional certification can also help enhance your credibility when you are starting out, especially if you have little or no related professional experience. Certified etiquette trainers may also demand higher fees.

There are a variety of certification programs in etiquette and protocol consulting. These programs offer training in business, dining, international, and social etiquette and training for teaching etiquette to children and teens. Programs typically run two to five days or more in length and cost anywhere from $1,000 to $10,000. If you are starting your own business, don't forget that tuition and travel expenses are likely tax-deductible as a business expense.

North American Certification Programs

On the pages that follow you will find a list of programs, in alphabetical order, that you may want to look into. When evaluating a program, here are some questions you can ask.

- What is the trainer's background to teach etiquette consulting?
- What, if any, support will I get when I complete my training?
- What materials will I receive, and can I use them for my business? Will I receive any additional materials, such as sample training presentations, brochures and advertisements? When were these materials created? Are they updated? Will I receive any of my materials on CD?

NOTE: We cannot say whether any of the programs listed in this guide will be right for you. You are the only one who can make that decision. Program costs and other details can change, so make sure you confirm information about any program before registering.

The American School of Protocol

The American School of Protocol offers a five-day Train the Trainer program which instructs participants how to develop and manage a children's etiquette program. Participants will gain hands-on experience by working with and mentoring a child during training. Classes are held every few months in Atlanta, Georgia, and are limited to ten participants.

Website: **www.theamericanschoolofprotocol.net**

Phone: (404) 252-2245

At Ease, Inc.

At Ease, Inc., offers a specialized Asian Etiquette Certification Program. The three-day program covers such subjects as proper introductions, conversation topics, and appropriate conduct in meetings and public places. The program is held at an authentic Japanese-style hotel in the heart of San Francisco's Asian district, and participants get the opportunity to practice their skills at dinners and other outings all over town. Contact At Ease, Inc. for information regarding availabilty and prices.

Website: **www.corporateetiquette.com/certification/asianet.tmpl**

Phone: (800) 873-9909

Email: askus@ateaseinc.com

The Civility Group Etiquette Leadership Training Program

The "etiquette leadership" certification program is designed to prepare attendees to enter the world of etiquette training and/or build their etiquette business. The program fees range from $3,500 to $7,500 CDN plus GST. Sessions include some meals, 18 hours of training, all books and supplies, and a certificate. Classes are offered four times yearly in Canadian/U.S. locations. Sessions for 2006 include Toronto and Ottawa, Ont., and 2007 in Victoria, BC and Winnipeg, Man. Check website for upcoming sessions.

Website: **www.etiquetteladies.com**

Phone: 1-888-293-7561 or (204) 452-9699

Email: info@etiquetteladies.com

Diane Diehl Company Train the Trainer Certification

Diane Diehl Company has developed training for entrepreneurs interested in beginning or expanding their business in etiquette/protocol. They offer a traditional classroom setting, as well as online courses. The in-class course is three days, and focuses on one (1) of the following topics: International Protocols, Business and Social Protocols, or Petite Protocol for Youth. Graduates are awarded a Certificate of Merit. The cost for each three-day program is $4,500, and includes all materials and dining programs, but does not include travel or accommodations.

Website: **www.dianediehlcompany.com**

Phone: (949) 955-2000

Email: diane@dianediehlcompany.com

Etiquette and Leadership Institute (Children's Etiquette)

The Etiquette and Leadership Institute provides up-to-date, easy to present etiquette, dance and dining lessons that include activities focused on teaching children ages 8-22 to be courteous and respectful. Graduates leave the training certified to use the same materials used by The Etiquette and Leadership Institute and successful children's etiquette consultants worldwide. Week-long training is held in Athens, Georgia a couple of times a year, and costs $5,200.

Website: **www.etiquetteleadership.com**

Phone: (706) 769-5150 or 888-769-5150

Email: eli@etiquetteleadership.com

Etiquette Survival Group

Etiquette Survival Group offers one- and two-day Train the Trainer course taught by company founder and President Sue Fox. Scheduled twice a year in California and Texas, the courses include sales and marketing materials, guides to setting up and promoting your business, etiquette curricula, videos, etiquette books, workbooks, games, and a web-site template. The training also includes on-going coaching via phone and continued promotion of your business on the Etiquette Survival website. The cost is $1,800 for the one-day, and $3,500 for the two-day course.

Website: **www.etiquettesurvival.com**

Phone: (408) 399-7417 (Northern California)
(626) 974-5429 (Southern California)

Email: sfox@etiquettesurvival.com

Executive Mentoring and Coaching International American Business Etiquette Trainer's Association (ABETA)

Executive Mentoring and Coaching International offers a two-and-a-half day certification program to become an American Business Etiquette Trainer. You will receive materials and training in founder Phyllis Davis' style to use in your own etiquette consulting business. This training is focused on the topic of business etiquette training, so it does not include social and dining manners. However, it covers topics such as techno-etiquette and meetings. The cost to attend is $2,500, and participants will walk away with an ABETA certification. They also offer online virtual tutoring in Business Etiquette Training, a free sample tour of which can be viewed at **www.lightspeedvt.com/mycoach**

Website: **http://mycoach.com/ethics_abeta**

Phone: (800) 95-COACH
(702) 433-3268

Email: pdavis@mycoach.com

Global Protocol, Inc.

Global Protocol offers a five-day licensee/certification program covering Business Etiquette, Protocol, and Professional Presence. Classes are held several times per year in Chicago, Illinois, but each class is limited to 12 students. After completing the certification, you will gain access to Global Protocol's website forums, attend update training retreats, and utilize the advice hotline with founder, Gloria Petersen.

Website: **www.globalprotocol.com**

Phone: (773) 714-5043

Email: info@globalprotocol.com

Global Success Strategies, Inc.

Global Success Strategies, Inc. offers a Certificate in Etiquette and Fine Dining. Training programs take place three times a year in Palm Beach, Florida; Charlotte, North Carolina; San Francisco, California; and Toronto, Ontario. Each program lasts five days and covers techniques for working with clients, diplomacy strategies sales and marketing skills, business tools and skills, and communication topics. It also includes mentoring services for several months after completion of the program. Each program costs $8,000. Additionally, the new Certificate in Image and Etiquette takes place three times a year in Charlotte, North Carolina, is 10 days long, and costs $15,000.

Website: **www.gloriastarr.com** (scroll down to “Etiquette Certification” and select “Overview”)

Phone: (866) 239-2422

Email: info@gloriastarr.com

Protocol Advisors, Inc.

Protocol Advisors offers two different certification programs for etiquette consultants. The five-day Business Etiquette and International Protocol Consultant program is geared toward consultants wishing to start their own business. The three-day Business Etiquette Training program is intended to help corporate trainers who wish to present etiquette and protocol programs within their own organizations. The five-day program costs $6,500 per student, while the three-day program costs $4,500. All classes are held in Boston, Massachusetts.

Website: **www.protocoladvisors.com/training.html**

Phone: (617) 267-6950

Email: info@protocoladvisors.com

Protocol Professionals

Protocol Professionals offers a Protocol Certification Program, which consists of three one-day modules on International Protocol and Etiquette, American Business and Social Protocol, and Special Event Planning and Production. Class size is limited to eight students. Cost is $4,500 U.S., and classes are held in San Francisco, California, about twice a year.

Website: **www.protocolprofessionals.com** (click on “Training” then “International Protocol & Etiquette Certification”)

Phone: (415) 673-5311

Email: rsvp@protocolprofessionals.com

The Protocol School of Washington

This school offers two different certifications: Corporate Etiquette and International Protocol Consultant, and Protocol Officer Training Level 1. Graduates are provided with scripts, CD-ROMs, and illustrated workbooks, and enjoy ongoing support. Training for both of these certifications is five days, and is offered a few times a year in the Washington, DC area. Cost is $5,500 per participant. Check the website for current offerings.

Website: **www.psow.com**

Phone: (877) 766-3757

Email: info@psow.com

Professional Associations

As you may have noticed in some of the certification program descriptions above, completing an etiquette certification program may qualify you for membership in a professional association affiliated with that program, such as American Business Etiquette Trainer's Association or Etiquette Professionals International Association.

International Association of Protocol Consultants

The IAPC offers two levels of certification: Certified Protocol Consultant™ (CPC™) and Certified Protocol Officer™ (CPO™). Courses take place in Washington, DC. There are six steps to certification, four of which require fees ranging from $995 to $3295, with a $300 discount given per certification step for IASC members.

Website: **www.protocolconsultants.org** (click on "Certification")

Phone: (703) 759-4272

Email: information@protocolconsultants.org

International Society of Protocol and Etiquette Professionals

ISPEP offers professional certification for individuals who have learned through self-study or etiquette courses. They offer the Certified Protocol Professional (CPP) designation, with plans to offer courses for Certified Etiquette Professional (CEP) in the future. Certification exams are held twice per year and there is an $850 fee to take the exam.

Website: **www.ispep.org/certif.htm**

Phone: (301) 946-5265

Email: info@ispep.org

College Programs

Although colleges do not offer degree programs in etiquette consulting, most offer degrees or diplomas in related subjects such as international relations or public relations. You can search for U.S. colleges and degree programs at Peterson's Education Portal at **www.petersons.com**. For Canadian Universities and Colleges search **www.schoolfinder.com**.

You can also find a variety of relevant courses offered through college continuing education departments. Depending on the course, you may be able to attend a single class on a Saturday or take an evening class once a week for several weeks. Following are examples of the types of subjects that may help you in your etiquette consulting career. Phone local colleges and universities and ask for the continuing education department (or adult education) to find out what courses they are offering.

- Business
- Communications
- Customer Service or Sales
- International Relations
- Public Relations
- Train the Trainer

Of course it's also a good idea to take local etiquette courses, whether they're offered by local businesses or colleges. If your local college doesn't offer etiquette courses, see section 5.3.2 to learn how you can get hired to teach classes in etiquette.

2.3.2 Find a Mentor

Another way to learn etiquette consulting is to find a professional etiquette consultant who is willing to be your mentor. Princeton University's *WordNet* defines the word mentor as "a wise and trusted guide and advisor." A mentor can provide you with personal training in etiquette consulting to help you launch your own career.

Once you have identified an etiquette consultant who you would like to mentor you, approach them with a letter of introduction (see sample on next page). In your letter:

- Explain why you selected them as a potential mentor. It may be their success in an industry you are interested in or that you admire their presentation skills. Whatever the reason, let the potential mentor know why you chose them out of all the etiquette consultants. But don't ask a local etiquette consultant that you'll be competing with to mentor you, or you might get a frosty response. Look to an etiquette consultant in another city or town.

Sample Mentoring Request Letter

Jones Etiquette Consulting
Attn: Judy Jones
123 Any Street
Lincoln City, ME

May 1, 2007

Dear Ms. Judy Jones,

I recently had the opportunity to attend your seminar on communication etiquette at the Hanover House in Lincoln City. I was very impressed with your presentation and your ability to make the subject fun and entertaining. I have read about your success as an etiquette consultant and this is the reason for my letter. I am beginning an etiquette consulting business in Jackson City, about 150 miles from your city. I would like to ask if you would be willing to mentor me in this new career.

I know that you are very busy and very involved with your work with Children's Hospital, which is one more reason that I wanted you to be my mentor. You have such a heart for the community and manage to handle a successful business and still have time for civic work, which is something I strive to achieve as well.

I want to ensure you that being my mentor will not require an exhaustive effort on your part. I would like to be able to communicate with you via email — this would be only when I had specific questions or concerns about the business. I would also like the opportunity to call on you once a month to discuss business issues or, if your schedule allows, we could meet for lunch once a month for these discussions.

I have experience as a specialist in computer systems, and would be happy to offer my services to get your computer running smoothly in return for your mentoring time.

Thank you and I appreciate your consideration of this proposal. I will follow up with you next week.

Warm regards,
Polly Proper
Proper Etiquette Consulting

- Make a specific request. Don't just say you want them to be your mentor; explain what you are asking. Do you want to talk with them on the telephone once a week for 20 minutes? Do you want to meet with them once a month over lunch? Do you want to communicate with them on a weekly basis via email? Also, be open to their offer of an alternative method of contact, as you are the one asking for a favor. Some people shy away from mentoring because they fear it will take too much time or energy. Assure your potential mentor this isn't the case.

- Offer something back. While some etiquette consultants charge a fee for mentoring (see below), others will provide the service at no charge. However, there may be many demands on their time, so you can offer to refer her business locally, or you may have another skill that you can offer for her mentoring services. Maybe you are a computer whiz and can offer to set up her new computer network. Or maybe you can write great advertising copy, and offer to write her next brochure.

Mentoring for a Fee

As mentioned, some successful etiquette consultants offer mentoring or personal coaching services for a fee, including:

Gloria Starr, CEO of Global Success Strategies offers a three-month mentoring program by telephone. For $3,000, she will answer all your questions on how to start your business, increase your current business, attract clients, create your personal brand identity and position yourself for success.

Website: **www.gloriastarr.com/training.htm**

Email: expert@gloriastarr.com

Phone: (704) 596-9866

Sue Fox presents private or small group Etiquette Survival seminars offered and designed specifically for each need and goal. The training includes presentation skills, communications skills, sales and marketing materials, guides to setting up and promoting your business, etiquette curricula, videos, books, workbooks, multi-media presentation, etiquette games, and website. Pricing varies, but ranges from $300 per person (hour consultation) to $75 per person (2 hour group program) up to $3,000 for 6-8 hour full program.

Website: **www.etiquettesurvival.com**

Email: info@lettgroup.com

Phone: (408) 399-7417

Cynthia Lett offers a paid mentoring program as well. You will have access to Ms. Lett for three hours per month either by phone or email. If you are located in the Washington, DC area, you can meet face to face. Once a month you will have access to a one-hour teleseminar on subjects relevant to your business and to your success. You will also receive a free CD of the teleseminar to listen to at your convenience. Ms. Lett will interview experts on subjects you and other etiquette consultants request. Cost is $400 per month, with a three month initial commitment. It is open to professionals who are teaching etiquette to children, teens or adults in your own business. You must have been in business less than ten years.

Website: **www.lettgroup.com/Seminars.htm**

Phone: (301) 946-8208

Email: info@lettgroup.com

2.3.3 Volunteer Experience

Events

You can get practical experience in etiquette and protocol by volunteering for any event that will involve dignitaries. Opportunities to get hands-on experience range from local events attended by the mayor to international events such as the Olympic Games.

Non-profit groups are always looking for help on their fundraisers and galas, and you'll get the double benefit of helping a worthy cause while you hone your skills. This is also an excellent way to make contacts in the community to help you land paying work when you are ready.

You can find help in locating your community's non-profit groups through the Internet. GuideStar is a searchable database of more than 1.5 million

IRS-recognized non-profit organizations in the United States. Visit **www.guidestar.org** then click on "Advanced Search" to search by your city, state, and non-profit category (e.g. Arts, Environment, Health). CharityVillage has a similar database of Canadian non-profit organizations at **www.charityvillage.com** (after you click on "Enter", click on"Links to NPO's").

You might also contact your local Volunteer Center or Chamber of Commerce. Both of these organizations usually run a volunteer matching program and can help make the introductions you need to get involved.

Friends and Family

Another way to learn more about the etiquette consulting business is to offer your services to friends and family for free. This may give you the opportunity to provide coaching on dining etiquette, wedding etiquette, or doing business with someone from a different culture.

Friends and family might also be able to arrange for you to do etiquette presentations at their office or to an association they belong to. This gives you the opportunity to sharpen your skills through practice. Plus, you never know who might be in your audience. You could get your first paying job from a free offering.

Every time you do etiquette consulting for someone – even a friend or family member (with a different last name from yours)—ask for a letter of recommendation. Recommendation letters look particularly impressive if they are on letterhead, so ask for several copies on letterhead if possible.

When you ask for a letter, keep in mind that many people are busy so they are more likely to do what you ask if you can make it as easy as possible. To help get the kind of recommendation letter you want, and make the job easier on the person writing the letter, you could supply a list of points they might mention, including what you did, how helpful your advice was, and what the benefits of using your services were.

For example, if you helped someone get a business contract, make sure that point is mentioned in the recommendation letter. The specifics will depend on the particular job you did, but even a few glowing sentences can help you look good to clients and employers.

2.4 Work Experience

There are a variety of jobs that can help you learn the skills involved in etiquette consulting. These positions can help you earn a salary while learning this profession, and may give you practical experience that will be invaluable in attracting and working with clients once you start an etiquette consulting business.

If you look through the classifieds or a job website like Monster.com, you will rarely, if ever, find ads from employers looking to hire an "etiquette consultant." But don't let that discourage you. In this section you will get some practical ideas to help you learn etiquette consulting skills at your current job or find a new job related to etiquette consulting. If you are resourceful, you might even be able to create a full-time job as an in-house etiquette consultant.

When looking for opportunities with your present employer or another company, keep your eyes open for jobs that will let you learn and use the skills described earlier in this chapter. In particular, consider opportunities to work in any of the following areas:

- Customer Service
- Events (especially if they involve dignitaries or special guests)
- Hospitality
- International Relations
- Protocol
- Public Relations
- Training

We found a company looking for a trainer whose job would include training etiquette issues for $25,000 a year, and another company looking for someone with a background in international policy willing to start someone with the right background at $85,000. Most likely, you will find something between these two.

2.4.1 Types of Employers

The need for etiquette and protocol extends across virtually all industries. However, some types of employers are more likely to provide the opportunity to get experience in these areas.

Government Departments and Agencies

These employers provide many opportunities to work in protocol. An example of the type of work they do is described at the website of New York City's Office for Protocol:

> Currently, the Office for Protocol extends hospitality due to Heads of State/Government, distinguished visitors, and other dignitaries. The office serves as liaison between dignitaries and the Mayor with respect to requests for meetings and invitations to events. In addition, representation at occasional receptions and ceremonies may be provided.

The United States has the Office of Protocol, which, according to the official U.S. government website, "directly advises, assists, and supports the President of the United States, the Vice President, and the Secretary of State on official matters of national and international protocol, ensuring that the accepted rules of conduct in every capital of the world are implemented." You can find their website at **www.state.gov/s/cpr**.

The Canadian Office of Protocol plans and coordinates for large, official events in Canada and involving Canadians abroad. Their site is located at **www.dfait-maeci.gc.ca/protocol/services-en.asp**.

There are also protocol offices at the state, provincial, and local levels. However, not all have protocol departments. Instead, you may find the protocol function in your area is carried out by any of the following:

- Chamber of commerce
- Convention and visitor's bureau
- Economic development department
- Governor's office
- International affairs department

- Mayor's office
- Tourism board
- Visitor centers

In addition, any government agency that receives distinguished visitors such as heads of state or celebrities may need protocol personnel. One example is NASA's Marshall Space Flight Center which has a protocol officer on staff.

You may be able to track down local protocol offices with online and telephone research to departments and offices such as those listed above. Another option is order a copy of *The National Protocol Directory* which lists protocol offices, as well as consulates and embassies throughout the United States. It also includes provides protocol guidance and other relevant information. The latest edition (2005) is now available for $18. You can find a link to order it at **www.nyc.gov/html/unccp** (click on "Publications").

Corporations

Many corporations offer you the opportunity to develop skills and experience related to etiquette consulting. You can find relevant positions in a variety of departments, but two departments most companies have which are most likely to give you opportunities to develop your skills, are:

- **Public Relations:** This department interacts with the public or customers. Depending on the company, this department may have a different name such as Corporate Communications, Investor Relations, Public Affairs, or International Trade. Among other activities, this department may coach company representatives who are traveling abroad or host foreign officials invited to visit the company.

- **Human Resources:** In many companies the human resources department is responsible for training. They may also organize events such as banquets and arrange overseas travel.

Any company that does business overseas, in a variety of industries from natural resources to high technology, needs staff to assist with protocol. However, even smaller local companies may need help with etiquette. After all, any company that has a customer service or sales department (in other words, virtually all companies), could use training in areas such as telephone etiquette.

In particular, public companies (those listed on a stock exchange) are often under the microscope of shareholders and the media. Everyone employed by a public company, from the mail room employee to the CEO, represents this corporation. Knowing proper business etiquette and international protocol is essential in a competitive market. You can help employees and key officers brush up on these important skills.

There are a number of places to find links to top companies in the United States and Canada. At Hoovers, you can search for a specific company, or click on "Companies & Industries" to go to a page with a menu that allows you to browse a company directory or search by industries. The Fortune and Forbes sites list top companies in the U.S., while Report on Business lists top Canadian companies.

- *Hoovers.com*
  www.hoovers.com

- *Forbes Magazine*
  www.forbes.com/lists

- *Fortune.com*
  www.money.cnn.com/magazines/fortune/fortune500

- *Report on Business (Top Canadian Companies)*
  www.globeinvestor.com/series/top1000

Hospitality Industry

Hospitality is all about being a good host. This is a vibrant and exciting industry with work in countries around the globe. Hospitality businesses can use the services of an etiquette consultant to train their staff in issues of etiquette and international protocol.

For example, hotels and resorts cater to a wide array of guests from various countries and cultures. The staff must know how to set tables, how to serve properly, how to greet guests, international protocol, and much more. As a result, etiquette training skills are in high demand at many upscale hotels and resorts. Other hospital industry employers that may be a good match for your skills include country clubs, cruise lines, conference centers, convention centers, and tourist attractions.

Of course you can find hospitality industry employers in your city simply by checking the Yellow Pages or one of the following resources: The Official Travel Guide at **www.officialtravelguide.com** or SeaLetter Cruise Links at **www.sealetter.com/resource.html**

Other Possibilities

Any employer that operates globally or plans events involving dignitaries has a need for individuals trained in protocol. Examples include:

- Airports and port authorities
- Event planning companies
- The military
- Non-profit organizations
- Public relations agencies
- Sports organizations
- Universities

2.4.2 How to Find Job Openings

It would be wonderful if you could just open the want ads in your Sunday newspaper and see columns and columns of advertisements for etiquette consultants, but that just isn't the case.

Independent consultants have traditionally handled etiquette consulting, and it is only in the past few years that companies and organizations have begun to realize the benefits of having an etiquette consultant on the payroll. You can explore traditional job search avenues, but you should also consider unadvertised positions.

Get Experience with Your Current Employer

If you are currently employed, chances are your employer was one of the types of companies listed above. Even if you work for a small business, your company very likely has one or more people working in customer service, sales, or human resources. Any of these areas might give you the opportunity to get relevant experience. So what happens if you work in a different department?

One solution is to volunteer to help the department you want experience with. Although not everyone will accept an offer of help (some people are territorial, afraid of training someone who might take over their job, or simply don't want to share work they enjoy), you might be surprised at how many people will jump at the opportunity for assistance. As a result of downsizings, many departments are short-staffed. With pressure to increase sales, improve customer service, and expand into international markets, departments related to protocol and etiquette might be able to use a hand. There are a few things to keep in mind when volunteering to help these departments:

- Speak to the right person. In some cases it will be the head of the department. In other cases it will be someone who is currently doing a particular task, such as training or event planning.

- Unless you are able to persuade your employer to transfer you to that department, you will still be expected to do your regular job. If you are not willing to work for the other department on your own time (lunch hours, evenings, or even weekends), getting work experience in this way is probably not an option for you.

- Your offer is much more likely to be accepted if you state your willingness to do the work that other people dislike doing. If you are willing to file, photocopy, make coffee, or do whatever is needed, say so. There are plenty of people who want to do fun tasks such as training, making it tough for someone without experience to break in as a trainer. You will have very little competition if you offer to do the work others are not willing to do. Consider it "a foot in the door." Show that you have a positive attitude and are willing to do what it takes to get the job done. If you provide excellent value to the department, you could be offered a job doing what you want.

Instead of volunteering, another option is to create a new job within your company. For example, if your company is growing, chances are they will need training for new staff.

Create a New Job

If the job you want doesn't exist, you may be able to create it, either with your current employer or a new one. Jacqueline Whitmore, founder and director of The Protocol School of Palm Beach (etiquetteexpert.com), created her own job at the famous Breakers Hotel in Palm Beach, Florida. Once she had obtained etiquette training certification, she petitioned her boss to become the first protocol officer of the Breakers, and succeeded. You can read her success story in section 6.3.

If you want to create a job with a company that you don't currently work for, it may take more effort, but it is possible if you can show that you will give the employer more value than you cost. To do this, you will need to know what you can do for an employer that will outweigh the costs to the employer of hiring you. Here are some examples of things that employers see as "costs" when they hire a new employee:

- Your salary
- Your benefits
- Resources you'll need to do your job (e.g. computer, supplies)
- Time of other staff members to train you
- Time of your supervisor to oversee your work

As you can see, you will need to demonstrate to an employer that you would bring them more value than simply covering the cost of your salary. Here are some examples of things that employers may see as valuable:

- Increasing profits by getting more sales (this could be done through etiquette training of sales staff or helping the company expand to international markets)
- Increasing profits by reducing the company's costs (for example, if your training of customer service representatives can help the company stop losing sales)

- Freeing up your boss's time so she can do more important work
- Reducing your boss's frustration by doing tasks he doesn't like doing himself

TIP: Although most etiquette consultants work alone, with the approach described above, you might even be able to convince a professional etiquette consultant to hire you as their assistant if you can convince them that, with your help, they could do more of the tasks they enjoy and fewer of the tasks they don't enjoy, while being able to take on more clients and earn more money.

Who to Contact

To decide which companies to apply to, keep up with local news. Read the business pages of daily newspapers and watch the TV news to find out what companies in your area need, so you can determine how you can fill that need.

Is there a fast-growing company in your area? These companies are usually looking to be the best and the brightest in the field, and etiquette training can give them that little something extra that makes them stand out in a crowd. Is there a company that is focused on offering the best customer service? Having the best etiquette-trained employees means better customer service. Is there a company that is gearing up to expand? You can offer international protocol training and business etiquette.

To create a job for yourself, you will need to deal directly with someone who has the authority to hire new people. This does not mean contacting the human resources department of a large company, unless that is the department you want to work with. The human resources department fills positions that already exist. If you want to create a new position, you will need to speak with the appropriate department manager or, in the case of a smaller company, the owner of the company.

You will need to meet with this person and learn what they need to be able to figure out how you can create value for them. It's best if you can establish a relationship with someone through networking. However, you may even be able to create a job through cold calling. For example, here is the type of message you might leave on someone's voicemail:

> Hello *<name of potential employer>*, this is Annie Assistant. I am an experienced employee trainer, and would like to meet with you to discuss how I could help *<insert name of potential employer's company>* increase profits by having me train sales and customer service staff. Please call me at *<insert your phone number>* so we can schedule a time to meet. *(If you actually reach the person, simply change the last sentence to ask when would be a good time to meet.)*

If the company is looking to increase profits, as many companies are, this call is more likely to get returned than a call simply asking if there are any job openings. You may need to be persistent and make a lot of calls, but if what you are offering is something that will bring a company more value than it costs, you can create a job.

If a company is interested in being at the top of the market, then etiquette is important to that company. It is your job to point this out to prospective employers. During a meeting with the employer, you will need to provide convincing answers to these questions:

- Why should this company create a job just for you? Because your skills will help this company and its employees be more competitive in a very competitive industry.

- How will you and this job benefit the company? You will create and implement company-specific training on a variety of topics from business etiquette to phone skills.

- What do you bring to the table? This is where you match your skills to the employer's needs. For example, perhaps you are a dynamic trainer who can create and present training programs on a variety of subjects and you are also able to do one-on-one training for executives who need special attention.

For many people, creating their own job is simply too much work. After reading how much self-employed etiquette consultants can earn, you may be thinking "If I'm going to ask people to hire me, why don't I do it for training contracts worth thousands of dollars a day instead of asking for a job worth thousands of dollars a month?" If you don't want to create your own job, but would still like to get some relevant work experience, then you may want to consider applying for an advertised job.

Advertised Positions

At the start of this section you read that positions for "etiquette consultants" are rarely, if ever, advertised. In fact, there are related positions available. If you are looking for a job online, you might do a search for keywords such as:

- etiquette
- liaison (used in the hospitality industry more than other industries)
- international relations
- protocol
- trainer or training

However, be prepared to do some digging. Most of the results you'll get when searching for "protocol" are careers related to computer protocols. Likewise, the term "etiquette" may give you jobs that simply ask for someone with good telephone etiquette to work in a call center. You may be able to find the odd job that includes "etiquette training" in the job description. Here is an example from Monster.com for a sales trainer position:

> Sales Trainer opportunity available for person with minimum of two years proven sales training experience—preferably in education. Duties include mentoring, ongoing sales training, internal and external customer service training, and telephone techniques/etiquette training.

In addition to being able to search by keyword or job title, Monster and other job search websites allow you to post your resume and search for job openings by location and even by company. Most allow you to set up an alert so that you receive an email notice when a specific job is posted.

- *Monster.com*
  www.monster.com
- *CareerBuilder.com*
  www.careerbuilder.com
- *HotJobs.com*
  http://hotjobs.yahoo.com

In addition to job sites, most employers advertise job openings at their own websites. If there is no link for "jobs" or "careers" on the home page, click on the link for information about the company. That will usually take you to a page that includes a link to job postings.

Entry-Level Positions

As you saw from the sample Monster.com ad above, most of the positions that are directly related to etiquette consulting training will require previous experience. The requirements are even stricter for most protocol positions, which may require a minimum of a Bachelor's degree in International Relations, Public Relations or Business in addition to relevant experience.

If you don't have or want to get that level of education or experience, consider an entry-level position. Many protocol officer positions are filled by individuals who started as administrative or executive assistants and worked their way up in the organization.

2.4.3 Job Hunting Materials

Before you head out to get that new job, you need to make certain that all your job hunting materials are in order. Your abundant knowledge of etiquette and your gracious manner will make any hiring manager consider you for a job, but you have to get in the door before you can make this great first impression.

Your Resume

As you know, your resume is a professional document that presents your skills, experience, and education in a simple format. Many employers make a snap decision based on your resume, so create a professional-looking document that showcases your skills and your experience.

A resume should be based on the job you are applying for — there isn't a "one size fits all" resume. Every job is different and will require different skills and experience. Make sure that your resume highlights the skills and experience needed for the job you are applying for. Depending on the position, you might highlight any experience, education, or volunteer work related to:

- Business
- Communication skills
- Customer service
- Cultural diversity
- Event planning
- Hospitality
- Human resources
- International relations (have you ever traveled overseas?)
- Marketing
- Personal or executive assistant
- Public relations
- Sales
- Teaching
- Training other employees (most of us have done this at some point)

You don't need to fill your resume with every job you've ever held, but you do need to show that you have the skills the employer is looking for. How far you go back with your work history will depend on the amount of this history. Most employers are only looking for 10 years of work experience so try to keep your resume to one or two pages. Additional advice is offered at job search sites such as Monster.com. Visit **http://resume.monster.com**.

Your Cover Letter

The first thing a potential employer will see from you is your cover letter, so make it shine. Of course it should demonstrate your excellent etiquette in communicating, but here are a few additional tips:

- Keep it short. One page is the maximum.
- Sound excited about the job. You want your potential employer to know you truly want to teach etiquette to their staff, or speak to their group.

Sample Resume

Darla Diplomat
123 Anywhere Street
Anywhere, State
123-555-1212
Darla@anything.com

Etiquette Training Experience

- Created telephone etiquette workshops for the Local County School district
- Developed a customized business etiquette workshop for the Chamber of Commerce
- Created and presented a dining etiquette workshop for a local supper club
- Created and presented "Table Manners for Children" workshop for the local school district

Work and Volunteer Experience

2005 – present: Teaching assistant, ABC County School District

1999 – 2005: Stay at Home Mother / Homemaker

2001 – 2003: PTA Vice-president and fundraiser for school events

1997 – 1999: Human Resource assistant, ABC Bank

Education and Skills

Studied human resource management at ABC College

Completed dining etiquette course at Farmer Continuing Education campus

Completed business etiquette course at Farmer Continuing Education campus

Proficient with Microsoft Word, Excel, PowerPoint, and Outlook Express

- Sell yourself. Use your cover letter to show how your skills, experience, and talents are a perfect fit for this industry.
- Show that you have done some research on the company. Look at the sample cover letter on the next page for ideas.
- Send it to the right person, and double-check the spelling of the name. You don't want to misspell the hiring manager's name.
- Proofread, more than once. Check for spelling and grammar errors, and then have a friend or relative read your cover letter for accuracy and clarity. You want to make sure that your cover letter makes sense.

Other Materials

Along with your resume and cover letter, there are a couple of other items that you might want to prepare for a meeting with an employer.

Portfolio

A portfolio is a collection of samples of your work that you take to an interview. A portfolio can help you stand out from other applicants. It offers an employer proof that you have the skills to do the job.

If you have created several etiquette workshops and have supporting materials (like handouts that you gave to participants), you can assemble them into a portfolio. Section 5.2.4 explains how to create a portfolio.

References

You will need to have a list of references ready to hand to your prospective employers. Have three to five references who can speak about your abilities and accomplishments as an etiquette consultant. You don't want to list these on your resume, but do have them on a separate sheet of paper and on hand when you go for your interview. Make sure to include full names (and titles, if necessary), addresses, phone numbers, and email addresses.

Once you have landed the interview, follow the advice in section 5.4.2 on meeting with prospective employers about your consulting services. The techniques that can help you land contracts worth thousands of dollars a day can certainly help you land a job worth thousands of dollars a month.

Sample Cover Letter

Sally Sohire
ABC Company
123 Any Street
Town, State 12345

March 1, 2007

Dear Ms. Sohire,

I am writing to apply for the trainer position you advertised in the Lake City Gazette.

You are looking for someone to handle call center training for ABC company. I have the experience and skills you are looking for, and have created training workshops on telephone etiquette and customer service. I would welcome the opportunity to work with you at ABC Company to create customized training for your employees.

I have admired ABC Company's dedication to excellence and customer service, and was impressed that your company won the "Widget Maker of the Year" award in 2006. I truly believe that my skills as a trainer make me a perfect match for the job opening.

I hope to hear from you soon.

Darla Diplomat
123 Anywhere Street
Anywhere, State
123-555-1212
Darla@anything.com

3. The Art of Consulting

An etiquette consultant can provide an almost unlimited variety of services to a vast array of clients. After all, etiquette, manners, protocol – call it what you will – permeates every level of society and all of our social and business activities and interactions.

As a professional etiquette consultant you might teach etiquette to individuals and groups ranging from young children to seasoned businesspeople. How you handle each consultation will vary depending on your clients, their specific needs, and the particular etiquette skills you are teaching them.

3.1 Types of Consultations

While most consultants eventually gravitate toward a particular niche, such as specializing in corporate presentations or children's programs, it is important to recognize that you are likely to receive many different types of requests for your services. They will normally fall into one of the following two categories:

Individual Consultations

This type of consultation is also known by several other terms including personal coaching, private consultation, and one-on-one consultation. While this training is usually face-to-face, it may also be done over the telephone.

These consultations normally involve working with a single person, but in some cases you may consult with a couple or several family members at the same time. For example, you might meet with an engaged couple and one or more of their parents to discuss wedding etiquette. Individual consultations give you the chance to get to know your client better and to meet the specific needs of that client.

Group Presentations

A group training session can be for a small group of five or a large group of several hundred, depending on the needs and budget of the client and your specific preferences. Some etiquette consultants do not like to work with very large groups, while others prefer it.

Training a small group of people can be fun and rewarding for both you and your clients in the small group. This training takes advantage of the intimacy of a small group and allows for discussions and a variety of training from the lecture to role-playing.

Remember that group training is just not appropriate for some people. Maybe your client is a high-level executive and doesn't want their employees to know that they need etiquette training, or possibly there is an employee who needs some one-on-one attention. During the initial meeting with someone who might hire you to train their group, you can ask if there are any people who might prefer one-on-one training or who might require one-on-one training because of schedule conflicts.

Learning Styles

The types of training you offer will likely depend on the needs of your clients and the particular learning style of your client. As a professional etiquette consultant, you need to be comfortable with all learning styles and able to offer training that matches each of these styles. According to VARK (which stands for Visual, Aural, Read-Write, and Kinesthetic) methodology by Neil Fleming, there are four types of learners:

- Visual learners want to see what they are learning. Use visual aids such as charts, graphs, and graphics to hold their attention.

- Aural learners are more focused on what they hear. They enjoy lectures and discussion groups. Help aural learners by allowing them to interact with you and, if you are in a group setting, with others. Encourage discussions.

- Read-Write learners enjoy taking notes and jotting down what you are discussing. Help them by offering a variety of handouts and training that allows them to take notes.

- Kinesthetic learners are hands-on learners who enjoy combining a variety of experiences to meet their goal. Help them by offering role-playing and hands-on experience.

Many of your clients will exhibit more than one type of learning style. Being aware of how your client best learns can be beneficial to you as you develop the action plan to help your client achieve his goals. There is more information about VARK methodology and a free 13-question questionnaire online. Look at this website to get an idea of your personal learning style, as this is most likely the method you will want to train in. Go to **www.vark-learn.com** and click on "questionnaire".

3.2 Consultation with Individuals

When a client contacts you with an interest in personal etiquette training, you have to assess the client's needs, determine a plan of action, and follow through with it, keeping in mind time and budgetary concerns. You'll take the following steps in a private consultation:

- Set date and time of initial consultation.

- Send questionnaire to client as far in advance as possible before meeting.

- Confirm meeting and remind client to complete questionnaire — one to two days before the meeting.

- Attend meeting and ask follow up questions.

- Work with client to determine a goal, then break final goal into smaller, manageable goals.

- Write goals into the Action Plan (explained below).
- Identify skills needed to reach each goal, and put these skills on the Action Plan.
- Identify where your client can learn the necessary skills and write on the Action Plan.
- Determine dates for completing the different training, and enter on the Action Plan.
- Create a Training Plan based on training options and your client's goals.

3.2.1 The Needs-Assessment Questionnaire

Before your meeting with your client, start a client questionnaire to get your client thinking about what they want to accomplish. You can send this to the client before the meeting (or put it up on your website) and have them complete the questions. Have the client bring their answered questionnaire to your preliminary consultation. Then you can use the questionnaire to determine their specific needs.

TIP: If your client is seeking etiquette skills to enhance their business skills, consider adding some industry-specific questions to the questionnaire. This shows your client that you have researched their specific situation and have an understanding of their industry.

3.2.2 Preliminary Consultation

Explain to the client that the preliminary consultation is a time to work together to determine what they want to accomplish in etiquette training, and how you will help them achieve those goals. This is often referred to as a needs-assessment meeting.

The preliminary consultation can take place in your office, the client's office, your home, the client's home, or a public place like a coffee shop. Most etiquette consultants begin their business on a shoestring budget, which doesn't include office space inside of their home, but if you do have an office, this is an ideal space to meet.

This is a meeting where your client talks and you listen. Let your client tell you what they are looking for and listen for ways you can meet these needs. You should also make some observations of your own about what this client might need by noting details regarding their behavior and mannerisms.

Sample Client Needs-Assessment Questionnaire

Why do you want etiquette training?

Are you interested in general business etiquette?

Are you interested in dining etiquette?

Would you like to learn more about how to be a better conversationalist?

Is there a specific event coming up that you want to prepare for? If so, what is the event, when is the event and who will attend?

Are you comfortable in a formal event setting?

Do you entertain in your home often?

Do you go out with friends or business associates once a month or more?

Do you want to learn more about being a host or hostess?

Do you enjoy socializing in small groups? Large groups?

Do you want to learn more about international protocol? Is there a specific country or region you would like to focus on?

Are you comfortable at social events? If not, why not?

Do you feel secure at business meetings?

Are you comfortable speaking to groups of people?

Do you feel comfortable making introductions?

Do you want to learn more about phone and letter writing skills?

Are you confident in your etiquette skills?

In your meeting, review the needs-assessment questionnaire with your client. Ask follow up questions based on their requests in an unthreatening way, such as:

- Would you be interested in learning more about how to use email, voicemail, and other communications more effectively?
- Do you want to learn more about how to introduce business associates to one another?

The phrasing of these two questions allows the client the chance to request help in communication etiquette and business etiquette without having to admit that they are not well versed in these skills.

During this initial meeting, you should get a good idea of what the client's budget and timeline for training is, so you can make your proposal reasonable and attainable. Occasionally, you will have a client who wants to go from not knowing a soupspoon from a teaspoon to hosting an international dinner party overnight.

As a professional etiquette consultant you need to coach your client into understanding if something is just not possible. When a client makes an unreasonable demand, don't try to meet it. If you fail, your reputation will suffer. By offering an alternative to their request, you are still providing a service and if you can get them in for some training, they'll probably come back for more.

This information is the basis for your consultation services for this client. You need to know what your client wants to accomplish and you need to put those wants on paper for your client to see. This takes us to the next step in the process — developing an action plan.

3.2.3 Develop an Action Plan

Now that you know what your client wants to learn, you need to work as a team to create a plan that will make it possible for them to learn the skills they want, in the time frame and budget they have allowed. An action plan is simply a written statement that identifies what you want to accomplish and how you plan to accomplish it. You will take away the information you have gathered through initial consultation and put together a plan to present to the client.

Creating an action plan that meets all your client's wishes is a three-step process. First, you must determine what you wish to accomplish. Second, you must determine which skills your client will need to meet this goal and identify the training your client will need to make this happen. The final step to your action plan is determining a timeline to achieve the goals you've set.

Sample Action Plan

Goal: Host an international business dinner for 50 people

Start Date: February 1, 2007

Completion Date: June 5, 20007

Goal to Achieve	Skills Needed	Skill Training Options	Completion Date
Be comfortable at a formal dinner	Dining etiquette	Personal coaching with Etiquette Consultant	Feb 14, 2007
Understand how to introduce people at a formal dinner	Introduction skills	Personal coaching or a seminar or workshop	Feb 14, 2007
Learn business dinner protocol	Business and dining etiquette	Personal coaching or a seminar or workshop	March 1, 2007
Host a small business dinner	Hosting etiquette	Personal coaching or a seminar or workshop	April 23, 2007
Learn some phrases in the language of those attending your dinner	Foreign language training	Language class (if time permits) or personal coaching	June 1, 2007
Learn protocol of the country or region of those attending your dinner	International protocol	Personal coaching or personal research	June 1, 2007

Determine Goals

You've learned what your client wants to accomplish through a combination of the client meeting, the questionnaire, and the followup questions. This is the main goal you will set, with smaller goals along the way. Remember that your client's goals should be specific, measurable, attainable, relevant and time-based. For example, your client may want to host a business dinner for 50 people with many international guests, and while that can be the ultimate goal, you need to help the client break this down into smaller goals.

Goal 1: Learn dining etiquette

Goal 2: Learn business etiquette

Goal 3: Learn international etiquette for each country or region to be represented at the business dinner

Goal 4: Learn phrases from the foreign language(s) that may be spoken at the business dinner

Goal 5: Host a business dinner for a small group

Goal 6: Host a business dinner for 50 with many international guests

Assess the Training Needed

You need to decide what specific skills are needed to meet the goals you have set, and what training your client will require to attain these skills. Some they may already have, while some will require teaching. Make a list, such as:

- Business etiquette (general)
- Dining etiquette (general)
- Introduction protocol
- Hosting protocol
- Foreign language training x 3 languages
- International protocol x 3 countries

Once your client has identified their goals and the skills needed to achieve these goals, you will need to help them create the action plan of what will be accomplished.

Sample Training Plan

Date	Time	Training	Location	Type of Training
02-09-07	11 am	Dining etiquette training	XYZ Restaurant	Coaching
02-11-07	11 am	Dining etiquette training	ABC Restaurant	Coaching
02-11-07	6 pm	Conversational French	Community College	Classroom
02-16-07	10 am	Art of the Introduction	EFG Center	Workshop
02-16-07	6 pm	Conversational French	Community College	Classroom
02-18-07	7 pm	Dining etiquette training	XYZ Restaurant	Coaching
02-19-07	7 pm	Dining etiquette training	ABC Restaurant	Coaching
02-21-07	10 am	Learning Business Dinner Protocol	RST Conference Center	Workshop
02-23-07	6 pm	Conversational French	Community College	Classroom
02-25-07	6 pm	Conversational French	Community College	Classroom
02-28-07	12 pm	Learning Business Dinner Protocol	Your office	Coaching
03-01-07	6 pm	Conversational French	Community College	Classroom
03-08-07	6 pm	Conversational French	Community College	Classroom
03-12-07	6 pm	Conversational French	Community College	Classroom
03-15-07	6 pm	Conversational French	Community College	Classroom
03-16-07	2 pm	Learning French Protocol	Your office	Coaching
03-17-07	6 pm	Conversational French	Community College	Classroom
03-18-07	9 am	Learning French Protocol	Your Office	Coaching
03-22-07	6 pm	Conversational French	Community College	Classroom
03-24-07	6 pm	Conversational French	Community College	Classroom
03-28-07	10 am	Hosting etiquette	Your Office	Coaching
03-29-07	10 am	Hosting etiquette	Your Office	Coaching

3.2.4 Carrying Out the Training

To carry out the training you will first need to consider where the client will receive training in each skill. Possibly you don't speak French, so you'll have to find a local tutor or class. If you are pressed for time, you can outsource the non-etiquette training, such as languages, and focus on your niche or specialty. Even if you have the skills to teach all topics to the client, you don't want to spread yourself too thin. Section 4.4 has information about finding and dealing with contractors.

The next step is to create a training plan specifying where and when each part of the action plan will take place.

Coaching the Client

In the personal coaching sessions, you can use a variety of training methods ranging from hands-on experience (such as a dining tutorial where you discuss etiquette during a meal with the client) to printed handouts. Section 3.3.5 describes training techniques for groups that can be modified to fit almost any client and their particular needs.

While the client will likely want to hear your advice on all the topics they need to learn, you can assist them to practice their skills by using role-plays. Role-playing helps clients rehearse how they would act in real situations. For example, if they are nervous about a meeting with a new customer, you can play the customer. This gives them the opportunity to prepare for the meeting without worrying about making mistakes or saying the wrong thing because it's only practice. With this experience, they are likely to feel much more confident and capable of doing and saying the right thing during the actual meeting.

3.2.5 Working with Young People

Teaching etiquette to children is very different from teaching etiquette to adults. Children learn differently, respond differently, and react differently than adults. Also, training children in etiquette must involve the parents, or else all the child learns will be lost.

Working with children will require that you provide excellent credentials, stellar references, and a proven track record, particularly if you are considering offering your services to school districts or other organizations.

Needs-Assessment

Parents or caregivers play a very big part in etiquette training for children. First, they are the ones who see the need and want to meet it. It's not often that a child will decide they need to brush up on their manners. Parents or caregivers are also the ones who will hire you to train their child.

Determining the needs of a child will depend greatly on the child's parents. To be successful at teaching the child etiquette, you must have parents who are willing to offer reinforcement at home. Teaching a child the proper way to use a fork is only going to go so far, if they never have to use it this way at home.

Make it a part of your training to send home information on what you covered that day and the behaviors the children learned. Ask the parents to begin to immediately reinforce your training by encouraging their child to use this new skill.

Also, it is beneficial to have regular parent meetings, which can be just a couple of minutes before class once a month. You need to make certain that the parents know the training schedule and have a copy of it. You may also want to have a presentation day where the children serve the parents and show off all those new skills.

Use the questionnaire on the facing page to get you started determining the needs of your youngest clients.

Age-Specific Training

Training for children is not like training for adults. Most children don't respond well to lectures, but they love role-plays. Finding the right teaching method for children will depend on the age of the children and the skill you are teaching them. Here is a breakdown of etiquette training based on age:

Ages 4-7

Children this age respond well to interactive teaching methods. Some etiquette consultants use puppets or storybook characters to teach the basics of etiquette. Etiquette specialist Dorothea Johnson has a series of books and workbooks featuring Catherine the Mannerly Cat that she uses when working with children. Johnson says the children adore the cat, and this makes the training fun and easy to enjoy.

Ages 8-12

These are the tweens — not truly children, but not yet teens. These are the children who will enjoy working in groups and acting out role-plays. You can find these children are funny and silly one moment and very grown up the next. Teaching this age group requires that you respect them and not talk down to them. You are also dealing with a group of highly emotional individuals, so your training should be adjusted as much as possible to meet the specific needs of each individual child.

Ages 13 and Up

This age group knows the value of good manners, but they often will act as if they don't care. These young teens are best dealt with on the level you would deal with an adult, but remember they still have many of the thought processes of children. Teaching this age group can be done with examples (humor is always a hit) and some role-plays.

Sample Parent and Child Questionnaire

Questions for Parents

Why do you want etiquette training for your child? Is there a specific event coming up that you want your child prepared for? Or do you want to increase his or her general etiquette knowledge?

Do you want your child to learn dining etiquette (manners)?

Do you want your child to learn to answer the phone?

Are you interested in your child learning how to introduce people?

Do you want your child to learn how to be a host or hostess?

Are you willing to reinforce at home what your child learns?

Are you interested in working with your child to teach him or her proper etiquette?

Do you want your child to learn about gracious gift giving, receiving, and thank-you notes?

Questions for Children

Are you interested in learning more about good manners?

Do you want to come to class each week and have fun learning about good manners?

Will you work hard and try to remember the things you learn?

Will you practice at home?

Will you be kind and nice to the others in your class?

Do you promise to have fun learning about manners?

3.3 Corporate Consultations

Most of your work with companies and corporations will be different from working one-on-one with someone. You'll have to handle your relationship differently and you'll have to report to someone who may not even come to the training sessions. However, this is great work to get. Not only will you earn money training groups of clients, but you'll be in front of many possible future individual clients.

Chapter 5 goes through the process of finding and contacting potential business clients, and presenting a proposal to get their business. Once a client has expressed interest in your services, here is the process of etiquette consulting for businesses.

3.3.1 Conduct a Needs Analysis

Many employers offer in-house education for their staff. While some sessions simply involve topics of general interest, usually you are consulted because there is some area of deficiency or difficulty. Corporations often find it more expedient to bring in an expert than to try to resolve the problem internally – especially when it involves a particularly delicate situation.

For instance, you may be asked to counsel staff on appropriate office attire. This is a burgeoning area of concern for employers with the advent of "business casual." Personal hygiene is often a factor here as well. It's awkward for a supervisor to address a person's body odor problem or the excessive use of perfume or makeup – but a consultant can approach the subject objectively and diplomatically, without the embarrassment of having to subsequently associate with that person.

You may find that particular industries or professions typically request certain types of programs. For example, health care organizations are often interested in patient relations programs. They may want a presentation for support and clinical staff covering such areas as treating the patient with dignity (addressing them by surname unless invited to use the first name), respecting privacy (not discussing a case in any public area), or perhaps cultural courtesy (recognizing that different customs and expectations can affect the patient's perception of his treatment).

In any industry, training sessions for front line personnel – including receptionists and administrative assistants – are a frequent request. A first impression made by telephone or in person is often the deciding factor in whether a client chooses to do business with that organization. Corporations recognize that staff with "advanced etiquette training" will represent the firm in a superior manner. They address people politely, know how to listen, and provide service in the most efficient, expedient, and diplomatic way possible.

For sales representatives, topics of interest include courteous delivery of marketing strategies and advertising (proper training of telephone solicitors, the dangers of "trashing" the competition or using misleading language); general business etiquette (the correct use of business cards, professional correspondence, procedure for business meetings), and business entertaining and dining skills.

While this can help you prepare suggestions for programs that are likely to be appropriate for the particular organization and employees who will be trained, it is important to remember that each client's needs are unique. You will therefore need to conduct a needs analysis to determine exactly what those needs are.

The best way to do this is to start with a list of questions you can ask clients to determine why they want an etiquette training program, and which particular topics they are most interested in. You will find a list of sample questions on the next page and can add other questions based on the information you received from the client during your initial conversation.

> TIP: It's even better if you can customize the questionnaire to fit that specific industry or company. To use the example of a health care organization, you would refer to patients instead of clients.

You will then arrange a meeting with the client to go over the questions and determine what their specific needs are. Don't forget to bring a pen, paper and time-planner to the meeting so you can plan out the training process, and business cards to hand out to all who attend.

Sample Questionnaire for a Corporate Needs Analysis

Why do you want to train your employees in etiquette?

Are there specific problems you are trying to address?

Do you want to train all employees, or just specific sections?

Would you be interested in customized and specialized training for each area of your company?

Are there any specific employees you feel would benefit more from personalized training?

Would you like your employees to learn how to communicate with clients or co-workers more effectively?

Is there a specific skill (such as how to introduce people, how to shake hands properly, how to host a business dinner) that you would like your employees to learn?

Have your employees had similar training before? Was it effective?

Would you like employees to learn more about telephone and email etiquette?

Are you interested in teaching your executives formal dining and dinner party etiquette?

Would you like your employees to learn basic business etiquette?

Is your company doing business with any international clients?

Are you interested in training your key employees in international etiquette?

What results would you look for to consider this training a success?

Begin your meeting by reviewing the questionnaire, then use follow-up questions to sell your services. For example:

- Mr. Whyte, you indicated that you'd like your employees to learn more about telephone and email etiquette. Would you be interested in having a customized telephone etiquette training program created for the company?
- Mr. Smith, you indicated that you've recently started doing business with a Japanese company. Are you interested in having an intensive Japanese protocol training program created for your employees who will be interacting with your new clients?
- Ms. Jones, you stated that you want your executives to learn more about dining etiquette. I know many of your assistant branch managers are promoted to branch managers. Would you like to include everyone from assistant branch manager and up in that training?

Once you've determined the needs of your corporate client, you will then complete an action plan and training schedule, just like you did for the individual client. Use the sample action plan provided earlier (see section 3.2.3) for reference. You may also incorporate elements of your proposal (see section 5.4) into your action plan.

Once you have your action plan in place and have developed your training schedule, you'll need to choose a topic (your clients may have a few options in mind), choose a date (often done as part of your action plan), and select a venue to present in. Let's take a look at these preliminary steps.

3.3.2 Choose a Topic

Corporations call in etiquette consultants when they have a problem they want to solve. Therefore, if a corporation wants you to present a training program for employees, they will almost certainly have a specific topic in mind. For example, a corporation that is experiencing a high level of customer complaints may ask you to present a training program on telephone etiquette.

If they tell you they want a presentation on telephone etiquette, find out why. Have they received complaints from callers? Are there specific behaviors the company wants to change? Perhaps they want staff to start addressing customers by their title and surname, rather than first name. Maybe some employees are using inappropriate language. Are they chewing gum or making other distracting noises when they're on the phone? The more information you have about the company's needs, the better able you will be to develop a program that meets those needs.

When presenting in a corporate setting, you will need to customize your training to the company specifics. For example, if the company has a standard phone greeting that is required by all employees, you need to incorporate that greeting into your business communication program.

Other corporate employers, such as convention planners, service clubs, and professional associations, are much less likely to have a specific topic in mind when they contact you. Instead, they may say they're interested in "something on business etiquette" and ask you to suggest a suitable topic. At this point it is up to you to recommend one or more topics that you think would interest their members. Section 3.4 covers a variety of training topic areas.

When narrowing down your list of topics, focus on what will appeal to people attending the particular event. For example, a group of salespeople would be much more interested in a presentation on dining etiquette so they can make a good impression on the people they're selling to, than a talk on wedding etiquette...unless, of course, they are salespeople in the wedding industry!

Your topic will also be determined to some extent by the amount of time you have available for your presentation. If a company wants to hire you for a one-day training program, your topic might be a broad one such as "Business Etiquette" and cover a variety of subjects. However, if you are asked to present a 20-minute luncheon speech, you will need to have a much narrower topic, such as "Cell Phone Dos and Don'ts."

3.3.3 Decide When and Where It Will Take Place

Choosing a Date

Usually the event organizer will have a specific date in mind when they contact you. For example, a convention organizer may be looking to fill a specific time slot, or a corporation may have chosen a date that fits with the schedules of everyone who would be attending. In such cases, they will ask if you are available for a specific day and time, so you can check your own schedule.

You may be asked to present your training in a one-day event, or you may be asked to present a variety of workshops over the course of several days. If you are hired by a large company to present seminars to their employees, then you will likely offer your seminars over the course of several days or weeks. You may choose to do your programs back to back in just a couple of days or you may be scheduled to present each day at a specific time.

In other cases, you may have your choice of dates or times. For example, many service clubs have speakers every month, so if the date they're calling about doesn't fit with your schedule, you can let them know you would be available next month.

Sometimes, the organizer may know they want to put on an etiquette program, but not have a specific date in mind. In that case, the following tips may be helpful:

- You can hold seminars at almost any time of the year; however, you should avoid late December because people are busy with the holiday season. You should also stay away from any statutory holidays and avoid competing with popular local events.

- If you are presenting a training program for a corporation, it can be held any weekday during business hours (or during a lunch hour).

- If your presentation is a keynote or feature speech as part of a larger conference, you will attract the largest attendance if you present it during a breakfast or lunch meeting.

Selecting a Venue

Another consideration is where you'll present your training. The company may have an onsite facility for you to use or you may need to find something else. For example, service clubs usually hold their meetings in the same location, while a corporation may have a training center that they want to use.

If you are asked to present a training program for a corporation that does not have its own training facility, you may want to suggest they hold the event off-site, at a hotel or convention center. These facilities have employees who specialize in handling details such as suggesting room layouts, arranging for audio-visual equipment, and generally helping you deliver a professionally presented event. Off-site facilities also have fewer distractions, so employees can focus on the training program.

Of course, this is only a wise idea if the company is willing to pay the cost of renting the facility on top of your fee. If they are not willing to pay extra to rent a venue, arrange to use a meeting room at their company office.

Taking your training to your client's office is often perceived as an added value service. Coming to your client's place of business cuts down on any down time that he would have traveling to training. Consider this when you set your fees. Also, make certain to visit the facility and check out the room or space they are providing you for training. You don't want to show up for training and find yourself in an unheated storage building in a winter storm in January.

To help you determine an appropriate location, use the training location checklist below.

Training Location Checklist

How many people will you be training?

Will you need access to electronic equipment?

How big of a space will you need?

How many tables and chairs do you need?

What is the cost of the training facility?

Do you need to provide snacks and drinks?

Will you need specific resources (such as dry erase boards, easels, access to copier, etc.)?

Venues for Dining Etiquette

If you are training dining etiquette it is likely that you will offer this training at a restaurant. Another option is to have the meal catered to either your office or your client's office. This will require that you have the appropriate dinnerware, glassware and silverware on hand or that you request this all be sent with the meal.

Another location to consider for the dining etiquette training is a private hotel dining room. High-end hotels have the appropriate dinnerware to provide you and your client with a formal dinner in a private setting. This gives you maximum privacy for training. However, you will pay for this privacy, so make sure the cost is passed on to the client in your fees.

3.3.4 Write Your Presentation

No matter how knowledgeable you are about etiquette, it is wise to prepare and practice your presentation in advance, rather than try to "wing it." Audiences appreciate presenters who make the effort of preparing a talk tailored to their specific needs.

Set Your Tone

Let's say you're presenting a seminar on communication skills to an accounting firm known to be conservative — in fact, all the accountants are required to wear a suit and tie to work every day. You might present a proposal on linen paper in a black folder and offer to do a short presentation on the benefits of communication skills focusing on communication among employees and clients. You might cover the need for using letterhead, the reasons for always including a business card in client communication, and the benefits of email.

Now, let's say that you're presenting the same topic to a computer tech company that is filled with employees who wear Birkenstocks and shorts to work, and have little client contact. Your presentation would then focus on communication between colleagues, and your presentation would likely be on PowerPoint with a simple handout. You may cover how to communicate with others, body language, and how to make email more effective. The key: Different companies, same workshop, different presentation.

Clients are looking for value in what you say and they are listening to make sure that you understand their specific situation or industry. A one-size-fits-all presentation may be easiest, but clients won't feel important. Creating a customized presentation will let your clients and potential clients know that you went the extra mile to create something specific to the industry or the company.

Speechwriting

Once you know what the organization wants, you can start selecting your material and writing your presentation. If you have ever given a speech in the past, you'll find the process is essentially the same for preparing an etiquette presentation. This section outlines a step-by-step process for writing a speech or presentation. You can find additional advice in the following free online resources:

- *Virtual Presentation Assistant*
  www2.ku.edu/~coms/virtual_assistant/vpa/vpa.htm

- *Tips: Researching, Writing & Performing Speeches*
  www.nvo.com/speechwriters/tipswritingperformingspeeches

- *Public Speaking and Presentation Skills Articles*
  www.fripp.com/articleslist.html#speak

- *Allyn & Bacon Public Speaking Website*
  http://wps.ablongman.com/ab_public_speaking_2

Organize Your Material

Organizing your material involves putting your information in order. Something that can assist you in this task is to use index cards (3" x 5" cards available from any stationery store). Write each separate point on a card. You can then easily rearrange the cards to ensure your presentation flows logically from one point to another.

Write Your Speech

Once you have put the points into a logical order, the next step for many presenters is to write out the complete body of your speech. (The body is everything except the introduction and conclusion.) When you give your presentation to an audience, you will not read it from a written manuscript, but at this stage writing it all out can help ensure that it sounds good.

The best way to carry out this step is to write your presentation as you speak it. In other words, don't sit down at a computer and silently begin typing. Instead, speak out loud (you can even record yourself) and type what you say. The result will be much more natural.

People speak at the rate of about 125-150 words per minute, so write the first draft based on this guideline. Remember that if you are presenting a seminar or training program, or anything longer than a 20-minute speech, allow time for group discussion and questions.

Add Transitions

As part of writing the body, you should add some transitions between each topic. Transitions are comments that let your audience know you are moving on to a new topic. They help your audience stay with you and keep them from getting confused, as can happen when a presenter jumps from one topic to another.

A transition can be as simple as saying, "Now that we have covered X, let's take a look at Y." However, your speech will be more interesting if you can make one part of your speech flow into another. You can find tips on how to write transitions using the resources at the end of this section.

Write Your Opening and Closing

After you have written the body, you can write an opening and closing that will fit with the rest of the presentation. (These may also be referred to as the "introduction" and "conclusion.") The opening should help to get the audience's attention, establish your credibility, and lead into your talk. The closing can wrap up your presentation and leave your audience on a high point.

There are many ways to begin a presentation, and of course you can use anything that works well for you. However, if you have not given many presentations, and aren't sure how to begin, here are some ideas that can be very effective.

At the start of the program it is a good idea to let people know what benefits they will receive from the presentation. In other words, tell them

"What's in it for you." For example, after introducing yourself and the topic, you might say something like: "Today I'll share with you some information to help you better understand people, have better relationships, and get better results." For children, you could give some specific examples, such as: "This information can help you get along better with teachers, your parents, and other kids." Then ask for examples of how that would be helpful to them.

The beginning of the presentation is also a good time to acknowledge your audience and, if appropriate, encourage participation. You might say something like this (put into your own words so it sounds natural):

> "I don't assume that this subject is new to everyone. If you're like most groups, there are probably many people in this room who are knowledgeable about etiquette, and possibly even some etiquette experts. When we get to a topic that you have experience with, we'd appreciate hearing your advice."

Edit It

Editing can make the difference between an adequate presentation and an outstanding one. Once your presentation is written, practice delivering it. This will show you whether it is the right length, how well it flows, and whether anything sounds awkward. If something doesn't work, then cut it out.

It can be difficult to cut stories you enjoy out of a presentation. However, if they do not directly relate to the presentation, or if it is too long, you may have to sacrifice some of your material for the good of the presentation.

Put It in Point Form

The final stage is to rewrite your presentation in point form. Condense each main point into a few key words on index cards, or full-sized sheets of paper if you prefer. During your presentation you will refer to these points to keep you on track. Having your notes in point form can make your presentation much more natural and interesting to your audience than reading it word for word.

Of course, you will want to ensure that the points you make are detailed enough to trigger your memory, and you may want to write out complete sentences where you need to communicate specific details accurately.

3.3.5 Etiquette Training Exercises

In addition to deciding what you will teach during the training, you will need to decide how you will teach it.

Hands-On Experience and Role-Plays

This type of teaching lets people experience the actual skill firsthand. While you can certainly give a talk about dining etiquette, participants will learn a lot more with a "dining tutorial." This involves participants actually dining while you explain the different elements of the place setting and proper etiquette throughout the meal.

Phone etiquette is another good topic for hands-on training because it is easier to replicate the actual experience and offer guidance and insight along the way. You can offer real-life training along with role-playing opportunities to give your clients as much experience as possible.

However, hands-on training can be a bit intimidating for some, so know your client and don't push them into anything. If a client is hesitant to try the hands-on learning approach, try a different method.

Lectures

Lectures are more often used with large groups when you need to present either a large amount of information or a wide variety of information in a set time frame. Lectures are more than just you standing in the center of the stage. You can incorporate several different types of learning styles into a lecture, such as:

- Flow charts, graphs, and videos for the visual learner
- Facts, figures, and information for the aural learner
- Handouts and note-taking opportunity for the read-write learners
- Small group breakouts and role-playing for the kinesthetic learners

Sample Introductory Exercise

Here's a sample exercise you can use at the start of a presentation. After making your introductory comments you can give your audience an opportunity to discuss what they would like to get out of the presentation, and to identify how it can be valuable to them personally. For example, you could say:

> "Many of us have similar challenges with [state the topic, such as 'telephone etiquette']. Tell us what you think are some common problems and I'll start making a list on this flip chart. What are some common problems with [topic]?"

If your audience is slow to respond, be prepared with a couple of your own items to write on the list. Then ask "What else?" Thank everyone who contributes, and write each item on the list whether you think it is a good point or not. At this stage you are simply brainstorming, and encouraging further participation.

After a couple of minutes of brainstorming as a group, you can ask them to break into small groups of about five people. You can introduce an exercise such as the following:

> "In this activity, you're going to identify the top three problems you're experiencing that you would like to find some solutions to today. You can use items on this list (point to flip chart) or come up with other items. You'll have about 10 minutes to discuss this. Please choose a representative of your group to present your list to the rest of us."

When the exercise is done, have each small group's representative present their list to the entire group, while you write down what they came up with. Then explain how the problems will be addressed during your presentation. If something comes up that isn't on your agenda, let them know you will allow some time at the end of the session for additional group discussion so their concerns can be addressed.

As you saw from the activity above, one of the best ways to make your presentation both interesting and relevant to participants is with audience participation. Throughout the program you can encourage participants to ask questions and share examples from their own experiences.

You can have participation either in small groups or with the entire group. For example, you might suggest that small groups of three to five discuss experiences where they have encountered a particular rude situation, how that made them feel, and what the result was. For example, if they encountered rudeness from a representative of a company, they might have decided to take their business elsewhere.

Resources

If you have previous experience presenting training programs, you may already have plenty of ideas for additional exercises you can create for your etiquette presentations. If not, one way to get exercises and materials is by taking an etiquette certification program as discussed in section 2.3.1.

However, if you don't plan to take an etiquette certification program and prefer not to develop all your own exercises and handouts, another option is to purchase training materials that have been developed by someone else. The following organizations sell training materials for etiquette consultants. Check with them for current prices.

- *Deal With It*
  Offers an Etiquette and Decorum training game with 108 situations and questions to present to your trainees. The module costs $89.
  www.uniquetraining.com/sampleetiquette.html

- *Etiquette Ladies*
  Offers a variety of Etiquette Training Program materials for anyone from age 5 to corporate executives. The program cost varies from $240 to $605.
  www.etiquetteladies.com/pdf/Affiliate_Package.pdf

- *Etiquette Survival*
  Offers an Educator Kit ($550) which contains curriculum materials you can use to train anyone from third graders to corporate executives. Also offered is a Business Kit for $1,295 which includes all materials in the Educator Kit, plus a "Getting Started Manual" with materials for an etiquette consulting business including sample marketing documents for your specialty (i.e. dining etiquette, business etiquette, etc.). Also included with the Business Kit is coaching with company owner Sue Fox. The company also offers videos on dining etiquette at prices ranging from $10.95 to $39.95 per video. New for 2006 is a Corporate Kit ($1,495) with training and materials specifically designed for in-house corporate trainers.
  www.etiquettesurvival.com

- *Manners International*
  Offers instructional videos and training kits for children, teens, and adults. Subjects include table manners, business etiquette, and social graces. Prices range from $24.95 for videos and accessories to nearly $275 for complete etiquette kits.
  www.mannersinternational.com/products.asp

- *The Proper Thing*
  Offers booklets on several topics, from basic business etiquette to customer service protocol to gender-specific advice on professionalism. Most booklets cost $6.95 or $7.95 each.
  www.theproperthing.com/books.htm

- *Protocol Consultants International*
  Offers a 20-minute video titled "Executive Etiquette – First Impressions" that covers such topics as handshaking, conversation skills, personal space, and so on. The video costs $74.95.
  www.protocolconsultants.com/videoorder.html

3.3.6 Prepare Materials and Supplies

Once you know what you are going to include in your presentation, you can determine the support materials you will need. If you aren't purchasing training materials, you will need to create them yourself.

Materials for Participants

Participants appreciate having something to take away with them at the end of a presentation. If you are giving a speech, you might have a one-page handout of etiquette tips. (This can also be an excellent marketing tool as well, so remember to include your contact information at the bottom.) For a training program, you could prepare several handouts. Other options are to offer a booklet (8 1/2" x 11" sheets folded in half and stapled in the middle) or a binder with pages of detailed etiquette advice.

In general, your materials should summarize the topics you spoke on, and possibly offer step-by-step instruction for implementing your advice in the corporate setting it was intended for. Sometimes the written materials will cover topics of interest that didn't make it into your presentation due to time constraints. If you have doubts about your creative abilities, hire someone to create your written materials.

TIP: If you take a training seminar in etiquette consulting, some programs offer the benefit of providing you with materials you can photocopy and use in your own training seminars.

- Picture of a table setting with all the pieces identified
- Sample list of common dining mistakes
- A dos and don'ts list on any subject you have discussed
- List of the proper forms of address
- Business etiquette guidelines including how to make an introduction and a proper handshake
- Telephone etiquette tips

It's also wise to print up an evaluation form that audience members can fill out just before leaving. You can use this feedback to fine-tune your presentation for next time, and to solicit testimonials to use in your promotional materials (see section 5.4.3).

The choice of how elaborate to make your materials will depend on whether the organization will copy them for you, and what they are paying you. For example, if you are being paid thousands of dollars to present a training program, an organization will usually expect you to provide participant materials and binders. If you are giving a speech for several hundred dollars, an organization may copy a handout for you.

Give yourself ample time to develop handouts for the presentation, and make sure that your business name and contact number is located on each page. Also, have your handouts printed and ready to go as early as possible. If your registration deadline is ten days in advance, then you can have your materials printed at least five days before your seminar.

Other Materials and Supplies

What you will need for your program will vary, but it is wise to develop a checklist of what you need in advance so you can make sure you have everything before the event.

Some items may be supplied by the facility you're using, some by the event organizer, and others you may need to supply yourself. For example, the event organizer or facility may provide:

- Paper and pens for participants
- Refreshments (water, coffee, tea, juice)
- Overhead projector
- Flipchart and markers

TIP: While PowerPoint may work well for certain types of short presentations in a corporate environment (e.g. a financial report for a board of directors), it is not recommended for a seminar or training program because speakers tend to be less dynamic and audiences participate less when PowerPoint is used.

To ensure the training program goes as planned, you should specify exactly how you want the room set up and what equipment you want. Section 5.3.3 has a room setup checklist for presenting your own seminars which you can also use for corporate training programs.

When you are scheduling the event, ask to have a representative of the organization available to oversee the room setup and arrangements such as refreshments and audio-visual equipment.

You should also try to have someone available to assist you during the event. This person could distribute handouts, track down hotel staff if you run out of coffee or the overhead projector breaks down, assist participants who need something, etc., so you can focus on delivering an outstanding presentation. But be prepared to do it all yourself if necessary!

Even if the organization has assigned someone to take care of everything for the training, bring extra markers, paper, and pens in case something comes up and the event organizer isn't able to attend. (It's also a good idea to have an extra copy of all participant materials and a backup plan for getting copies made if necessary.)

3.3.7 The Day of the Training Program

By the time training day arrives, everything should be in place for a fabulous event. Below is an overview of what to do that day to help everything go as smoothly as possible:

When	What
90 minutes before	Arrive at the location. This gives you a chance to catch your breath and get set up before people begin arriving.
60 minutes before	Double-check that all electronic equipment is in working order.
45 minutes before	Get the check-in table in order with materials to hand out and cards to fill out (if applicable).
30 minutes before	Begin to meet early birds.
15 minutes before	Go to podium area and do a final review of your notes.
Start time	Welcome the group and let them know how the training program will proceed. Let them know when breaks will take place (allow for 15 minutes at least every two hours plus lunch). Tell people to turn off any pagers or cell phones.
15 minutes in	Introduce material and review what you will be discussing today.
Halfway point	Break for specified period of time.
15 minutes before end	Let everyone know that you only have a few more minutes, but ask everyone if they will fill out the evaluation form that you will pass out at the end of class.
5 minutes before end	Hand out evaluation forms.
Ending time	Close class with a thank you.

3.3.8 Handling Difficult Situations

As an etiquette consultant you will be faced with a unique set of circumstances when making a presentation. While you very likely will have audience members that are looking forward to your presentation, others may not be as receptive, and it will be your job to win them over.

For example, many audience members may fear their lack of etiquette knowledge may make them look foolish if they speak up, while others may consider themselves etiquette "experts" who are ready to challenge what you say. If you are presenting a training program that employees are required to attend, you may have a number of participants who would rather not be there and don't understand why they "need" etiquette training. They may feel that attending an etiquette training implies they are boorish and impolite to begin with.

Fortunately, there are a number of techniques that can help win your audience over and make your presentation a success. According to our experts, one of the best ways to confront these challenges is by being the opposite of what people expect. By challenging their expectations of what an etiquette consultant might be (a school-marmish little old lady dressed in black with a severe bun, perhaps) you will challenge their beliefs on etiquette.

To this end, you will need to develop a training style that is engaging and that makes this topic fun. Exuding your own enthusiasm for etiquette and its benefits can result in an audience that responds enthusiastically. Earlier sections of this guide explained how to include interesting activities for participants (section 3.3.5) and develop a dynamic speaking style (see section 2.2.2). In this section we'll look at ways to deal with some specific challenges.

TIP: If possible, get involved in promoting the event and yourself in advance. This is especially a good idea if it is optional to attend. For example, to encourage registrations you might offer to write an article for the organization's newsletter. You can use this opportunity to generate interest in your training and set a tone that is fun and engaging.

Encouraging Audience Participation

For many people, speaking up in a group can be a scary experience. They don't want to risk sounding foolish, especially if co-workers or other people they respect are in the audience. Therefore, to get people to participate, you need to make it safe, and reward them for taking the risk of speaking up.

To make it safe, let people know participation is optional, even in small groups. For example, some people may not wish to discuss their feelings or share a personal experience, so you could say that if someone prefers not to discuss a personal situation, they can discuss a situation they have witnessed. During discussions, you can also validate people through the words you use and your tone of voice. See the list on page 39 of "Words that Help" and "Words that Hurt."

Dealing with Dissension

One of the best ways to minimize dissension is to acknowledge early in the presentation that there are differences of opinion about etiquette. What is considered acceptable behavior changes over time, and even etiquette experts sometimes disagree about what to do in a particular situation. For example, some say a verbal thank you is acceptable when receiving a gift, while others say thank yous should always be handwritten.

Also, as you will see from other examples in this guide, what is considered acceptable in one culture may not be acceptable in another. To cite an example given earlier in this guide, in some places it is considered rude to leave your shoes on after you enter someone's home, whereas people in other places would be shocked if you removed your shoes in their home.

You can also explain that many organizations and families have their own standards of behavior and even if others don't share those standards, those behaviors may be acceptable within those organizations or families. This is an important point to make, because you are likely to encounter participants whose parents have taught them certain ways of behaving that are contrary to accepted rules of etiquette. And arguing that someone's mother is "wrong" is not likely to go over well.

In fact, an excellent rule for dealing with adult groups is: "Don't make a participant wrong." Typically, when a participant is criticized, or told they are "wrong" by a trainer, other participants will empathize with the person criticized and feel anger towards the trainer.

During the group training session, if one person stands out to you as someone who needs special attention because they aren't comfortable working within a group or for any reason, then you can also suggest one-on-one training to the person or their supervisor. Also, consider handing out evaluation forms that have the option of requesting information for one-on-one training. Then you can follow up with this person away from the workplace.

When a Participant is Wrong

So what if someone says something that is clearly "wrong" during a training? For example, imagine a participant were to say: "My mother told me that after a meal at a restaurant or in someone's home, you should always use a toothpick while you're at the table to make sure you don't have any food stuck in your teeth."

In this case you might acknowledge that different families have different standards of behavior, but this is something etiquette experts say is generally not considered acceptable in North American culture, and to avoid giving offense, it is usually wise to do what is considered acceptable in the culture you're in. You could then turn it over to the group and ask if anyone else has an opinion or experience with this matter.

Very often, the rest of the group will let the person know what is commonly considered correct etiquette. If it turns out that everyone in the group disagrees with what is considered proper etiquette, you might say something like the following:

> "If you were dining with this group of people, it would be fine to behave this way. However, it may be helpful to realize that other people are not as open-minded as the people in this room, and might find that behavior inappropriate."

This compliments the people in the room, while making them aware of the reality that others would not find the behavior acceptable.

Responding to "Why Should I Change?"

Some participants will feel they should not have to change, and that others should accept them the way they are. You can reassure them that how they behave is their choice, and they don't have to change their behavior (unless, of course, their employer requires them to change). You could say something like:

> "This is simply information about behavior that can help if you'd like to have better relationships or get better results with people. It's up to you to decide if you will actually do any of these things."

Etiquette is about helping others feel more comfortable. When combined with explaining how etiquette can also benefit them personally, it can make them eager to learn.

3.4 Training Topics

The information in this section can serve as a starting point for the material you present in your coaching and training programs. Of course, you will need to customize the material to meet the needs of your own clients. The Resources chapter of this guide lists a variety of books that can assist you with further research on each topic.

3.4.1 Dining Etiquette

This topic is covered in depth in section 2.1.1.

3.4.2 Business Etiquette

Business etiquette covers more than just the basics of running a corporate meeting, greeting a new client, or hosting an after-hours social. It details a mode of conduct that will make those who have training in it stand out from their colleagues and competition.

As an etiquette consultant, you can teach business etiquette in a variety of ways, including lectures, worksheets, live action, and role-playing. People learn in different ways, so be prepared to adjust your training to meet the needs of your client. More information on learning styles appears in section 3.1.

Making Introductions

In a business setting, the highest-ranking person is introduced to others in order of their rank. For example, the regional manager is introduced to the CEO, then the branch manager is introduced to the CEO, and so on. The only exception to this rule is when a client is present — the client is always introduced first.

Never neglect to introduce someone who is standing with a group because they don't have the same rank as the others you are introducing; this isn't acceptable. While business introductions do follow rules of rank, these are never superceded by good manners and civility.

When you are making your introductions, always introduce a person by their first and last name and any appropriate title, such as doctor or general. It is never appropriate to introduce even a close associate by a first name only. The only people who are introduced by their first names are children. While the use of first names in the business setting is quite common and has become the norm in most industries, it is still best to wait until a person gives you permission before using their first name.

Women can be called Ms., Miss, or Mrs., depending on their marital status and their preference. If you find yourself in a position where you must immediately introduce a woman and you are unsure of her preference, use Ms. However, it is best to ask a woman her preference of titles in advance.

When you are in a smaller meeting, you can make mass introductions where you introduce the new CEO to everyone at the meeting, if this is a reasonable task. However, if the new CEO is attending the annual regional meeting with 50 people present, then you might want to skip the individual introductions unless you (and the visiting CEO) don't mind taking an hour or more on introductions.

At a minimum, you would introduce the higher-ranking attendees. This can be done before or after the meeting in a casual manner, or you may decide to have an "after the meeting" get-together for a small group.

When making introductions you will at some time forget a name. Just confess your momentary lapse with "I'm sorry, your name escapes me" and get the name. It may be embarrassing, but not introducing someone will look much worse than a case of forgetfulness. And remember to smile when you introduce people, as you'll look friendlier and more approachable.

Handshakes

Shaking hands is the accepted form of greeting in many countries. In North America, it is expected that a handshake be accompanied by eye contact. When you are introduced to someone it is proper to stand and extend your hand in greeting. Of course, there is always that occasion when you greet someone or are introduced to someone and your hands are full. In this case, it is acceptable to nod your head in greeting.

The North American handshake, for both men and women, is a firm, solid – but not bone-crushing – grip, with your hand placed fully into the other person's hand. The grip is followed by two to three small shakes (from the elbow, not from the shoulder) and then a quick release. This whole action lasts three to four seconds. (See section 3.4.3 for information on international protocol for handshaking.)

Traditional etiquette once dictated that a man never extended his hand to a woman when meeting. He had to wait for her to extend her hand for a handshake. Now, it is perfectly acceptable for a man to extend his hand to a woman or vice versa.

Handshakes are expected when you:

- Are introduced to someone new
- Greet someone entering your home or office
- Meet someone you know outside of your home or office
- See someone to the door
- Close a business deal or transaction
- Leave a function or event

Distributing Business Cards

Handing out your business cards is something that every good businessperson should do. You want and need your name out in the community, and what better way than with a card that carries all your contact information. Always keep business cards on hand, as you never know who you might run into.

Keeping your business cards in a case is much more professional than keeping them scattered across the bottom of your briefcase or bag. It will also ensure that you only hand out pristine cards. Who wants to receive a torn, worn, or stained card, and what is that saying about your business?

Business cards are considered a symbol of your status in many foreign countries, so if you are dealing with other cultures in your business, make certain that your title is printed boldly on your cards.

> **TIP:** Exchange your business cards before or after a meal. Don't begin dealing out business cards between courses.

Business Conversation

What to talk about in a business setting is often at the top of an etiquette client's list. So what do you talk about in a business setting? It depends on the type of business function and whom you are talking with. You wouldn't discuss the same topics with the company president that you would discuss with a close co-worker.

For a meeting or social event, take the time to review the guest list and learn a fact or two about each person attending. If this is a client or potential client, learn some facts about their company and some industry specifics. Also, if your guests are traveling from out of town, find out something about the area they are from. If you are entertaining international guests, make certain that you have brushed up on protocol of that country.

You can always open a conversation with "What do you do with the company?" if you are meeting someone for the first time. A simple "How long have you worked with the company?" is a good opener, as well. Also, try to make sure to ask open-ended questions that encourage conversation and try to respond to any questions with more than a yes or no answer. Other acceptable business topics include:

- **Current events:** Brush up on the latest news stories before your function.
- **Sporting or cultural events:** The local sports team or a new art exhibit make for good conversation. International sporting events, such as the Olympics, make good conversation for larger and more broad-based meetings.
- **Business news:** Stock is up or profit is up — always good conversation for business functions.
- **New books:** An internationally known book can make for good conversation.

Making conversation at a business function differs from making conversation at a family get-together. While catching up on the latest antics of your eccentric Aunt Bess and dishing the dirt on your wild cousin Bob may be fun, this type of gossip is completely inappropriate in a business setting. You don't want to tarnish your reputation by spreading gossip about a coworker or a client.

At a dinner, wait until the meal is complete and the dishes have all been cleared, and as your guests enjoy after-dinner drinks or coffee, you can start the business discussions. You may want to make a brief announcement or you may have a proposal to present. Whatever your plans, just remember that even in this relaxed atmosphere you are still doing business.

Email Etiquette

Email is a fast and easy way to correspond with business associates, friends, and family. However, while this technology makes it easy to keep in touch with everyone in your circle, there are rules to abide by:

- It is considerate to keep everyone's email address confidential. If you are sending an email message to a number of people, enter the recipients in the "blind carbon copy" (bcc:) section. That way the recipients and their email addresses are kept private from the other people receiving the message.

- Business email messages should be concise. The writer should always use proper grammar, spelling, punctuation, and sentence structure in every business email message. Some people type in all capital letters because it is easier and faster to do so. This comes off as shouting and can lead to misunderstandings.

- Before forwarding "informative" messages on to friends and colleagues, check to see if the information you are passing along is a hoax or authentic. Many people blindly forward hoax emails about companies that will reportedly pay you thousands of dollars to forward emails to everyone you know or a virus that puts a teddy bear icon on your computer. You can research the latest in technological urban legends at **www.snopes.com**.

- There is no such thing as absolute privacy. Email can be monitored by a corporate server or intercepted by skilled hackers. To be on the safe side, don't use email to discuss confidential matters.

- Avoid forwarding jokes or other "junk" email to business associates, as this creates a poor impression of your professionalism.

- Don't send attachments unless they are necessary. Large attachments can fill up a person's in-box quickly and, given the number of destructive viruses passed from computer to computer, people are generally wary about opening attachments.

- An easy way to connect with recipients is to attach a signature to the bottom of an email message. Including your phone and fax numbers, address, email address, name and position in each message makes it convenient for people to reach you.

- It is good practice to reply to each email message as soon as possible — within the first 24 hours, if not the same working day. Consider using an automated reply to let people know their message has been received and when you expect to reply personally. If the original message requires extra attention or research, send a quick note back explaining the situation and promising to respond as soon as you can. This lets the sender know you received the email and shows that you are giving the issue or question the time it deserves.

- Emailers should also be cautious when using priority markings for their messages. Unless a message is time-sensitive or urgent, avoid using those settings. Overusing the "high-priority" tag will annoy recipients and cause them to ignore this rating on all your messages.
- When composing a message, re-read what you have written before you send it off. Consider how your letter will be read, as sarcasm and dry wit don't transcend to the written word very well. Don't use email abbreviations (such as LOL for laughing out loud or L8R for later) for business correspondence, or with readers who may be unfamiliar with the references. And before you send it, check your spelling and grammar.

Meetings

If you work in a business that employs more than two people, then you will, at some point, attend a business meeting. There are several types of meetings, but the most common fall into three categories:

Office, Division, or Committee Meetings

These meetings are often informal, with close coworkers discussing a particular issue or set of issues. Some businesses have regular meetings just to keep everyone updated on what is happening in different areas of the business. This is a meeting that requires you to be attentive and participate, when appropriate, but don't take over the meeting with a list of your suggestions, complaints, or ideas. If you want to be heard, then ask the meeting facilitator to put you on the next meeting agenda.

Sales Presentation Meetings

Sales presentation meetings are a different breed than your typical office or division meeting. They also differ greatly from large corporate meetings, in that you are meeting with people outside of your company in an effort to gain their business. This is your meeting to shine, if that is what your job title allows. You may be called on to make a presentation or speak on a specific topic. Keep your presentation on target and to the given time limit, as going over your allotted time tells your clients that you don't care about their time constraints.

Large Corporate Meetings

Corporate meetings may come under the heading of annual corporate retreats or corporate strategy meetings, or some other similar title. No matter the title, if you are attending a meeting that includes associates from across the company, then you must be on your best behavior. Even if your annual retreat takes place in a mountain lodge or at a vacation beach spot, this isn't the time to let your hair down. This is business and all that it implies.

The hierarchy that rules your company is still in effect even when you are all away from the office. If your company president has always behaved very formally toward you and other employees, don't expect them to suddenly decide to buddy up.

For meetings, whether you are an administrative assistant or a vice president, there are rules of etiquette that must be followed:

- Remember that these meetings have a specific purpose, and it is good business etiquette to come prepared. Determine what you expect to achieve at your meeting. Will this meeting increase your knowledge? Or is this an opportunity to showcase your talents or skills?

- Always arrive on time, and silence your cell phone or pager at any meeting. Never interrupt anyone speaking, unless the building or the speaker is on fire (literally).

- Don't look at your watch every few minutes during the meeting. If you are rushed, don't attend the meeting or reschedule it.

- Make it a point to be polite and gracious to everyone at the meeting. Even if discussions get heated, keep your cool. Business meetings don't give anyone the opening to be anything but polite and civil.

Business Entertaining

Business isn't always done in an office or a boardroom. Many business deals are negotiated over a meal or at a social event. There may come a time when you are required to entertain a client or a potential client. You need to be prepared.

A nice restaurant may be the best choice for a business dinner, unless you are worried that other people will overhear your conversation. If this is the case, then you may decide on a restaurant or hotel with private dining rooms. Make certain that you provide a setting that is **comfortable** for your guests. Review your dinner options with dining etiquette in mind, and steer clear of meals that will be hard to consume politely.

As the host of the meal and meeting, it's your responsibility to arrive early and make sure your table or private dining room is ready. You may want to use place cards if you have many people attending; otherwise you will seat each guest yourself. Remember, the guest of honor or the most important (or highest ranking) guest should have the **best chair**, which is the chair that faces the door or the open restaurant.

You should ensure that guests are greeted at the entrance of the restaurant or hotel, and make certain that you introduce guests to one another. Also, let the waiter and the maitre d' know that you will be handling the check for the evening.

Cocktails are optional; however, use good judgment and exercise self-control. Also, if your clients don't order cocktails and you are unsure of their views on drinking alcohol, it is best to forego the drinks. If you don't drink alcoholic beverages, suggest that your clients order a cocktail before dinner and order a mineral water or some other beverage for yourself.

It is a good idea to let everyone know that business will be discussed after the meal is completed. This helps everyone to relax and enjoy the food. Make a brief announcement at the beginning of the meeting as to its purpose.

When the business is completed, make certain that you see your guests to the door of the restaurant, and thank them for their time and attention. Follow up the next day with a short note.

3.4.3 International Protocol

A lot of business today is conducted on a global scale, and as a result you may receive requests for international protocol lessons. You may also decide to develop an international etiquette seminar or workshop to market to companies and organizations in your area. The most important rule in international etiquette is not to assume that all cultures imitate, or even approve of, North American culture.

While everyone needs to have some knowledge of the protocol in different countries, it is especially important for those who are:

- Seeking employment with a foreign corporation
- Trying to market a product or service to a foreign corporation
- Hosting a foreigner in their home
- Working with an array of people of different nationalities
- Wanting to broaden horizons
- Planning to travel abroad

If a client contacts you to train them on the etiquette of a specific country or region you are completely unfamiliar with, it's best to be honest. You can offer to research and learn about the rules and customs of the region or you can also offer to bring in an expert consultant who specializes in that region.

While you can teach some international etiquette generalities, you will need to research the specifics on etiquette in the area, region, or country that client will be traveling to or doing business with. Here are some free and inexpensive resources to learn about different countries. Helpful books on international protocol can be found in Chapter 8.

- *CultureGrams*
  CultureGrams sells four-page reports about 187 countries with information on the unspoken rules for greeting people, gesturing, visiting, and eating, among other topics. You can download the information online for $4 per report.
  www.culturegrams.com

- *Culture Briefings*
  A source of information about several countries, prices from $9.95 to $11.95.
  www.culturebriefings.com

- *ExecutivePlanet.com*
  A great resource for business travelers. It offers free reports on the culture, customs and protocol of dozens of countries.
  www.executiveplanet.com

- *The International Business Etiquette Sourcebook*
  Free information from the government of Canada. Scroll down to find a particular country.
  http://atn-riae.agr.ca/export/4027_e.htm

- *Worldwide Business Reports*
  BusinessCulture.com publishes a series of reports on doing business in particular countries, including business customs, etiquette, cross-cultural communication, proper gifts, negotiating tactics, business culture, manners, business entertainment and more. Prices start at $18 per report.
  www.businessculture.com

Rank, Status, and Forms of Address

Doing business internationally means you may need to address royalty, political officials, or ambassadors. Remember to research the specifics of the country you will be hosting or visiting.

In some cases you may not know which name is a first name and which is a second name, so make sure you find out in advance — some countries place the surname first.

Royalty

European royalty has a king and queen who are referred to as "Your Majesty" in conversation. Once you have spoken for a few minutes, you can switch to "Sir" or Ma'am." When you introduce a king or queen, say "His Majesty, the King" or "Her Majesty, the Queen."

Of course, there are more than just kings and queens. There are dukes, counts, knights, princesses, and many other titles to learn. A good place to get a list of titles and ranks is from the American embassy in the specific country you are researching.

There are also certain rules of etiquette when meeting royalty face-to-face. You don't extend your hand to a member of the royal family; you let them extend their hand first. Subjects of the royal family should curtsey or bow in the presence of their country's royal family; U.S. and Canadian citizens aren't required to do so, but you may bow or curtsey if you wish.

Ambassadors, Heads of State, and Other Officials

European heads of state, cabinet officers, ambassadors and other heads of state are referred to as "His Excellency" or "Her Excellency." If you were writing a letter to one of these you would address the letter (for instance) "His Excellency, the Ambassador of Nigeria." Other possibilities are "Your Grace" (a religious honorific), "the Honorable" (for judges and politicians), or by profession, as some countries prefer.

Interacting With Other Cultures

In the U.S. and Canada we believe in a firm handshake, a hearty greeting, and direct eye contact. But this isn't the way in every country you will visit or do business with.

Making Introductions

Before you head out on international business, make it a point to have your title boldly printed on your cards. Many countries are very status and rank-conscious… in fact, in some countries your status can even dictate how you are addressed. Also, consider having one side of your business cards printed in the language of the country you are visiting.

In presenting and accepting business cards, some countries believe you should study and review a card, others believe cards should be accepted and immediately put away. There may also be region-specific rules for presentation, such as which hand it is to be presented with.

Handshakes

Not every country believes in the firm handshake that is the norm for North Americans. In fact, in France the handshake is anything but hearty. Some countries don't believe in handshaking and prefer to kiss on the cheek or to air kiss. Other countries consider any kind of physical contact taboo.

Eye Contact

Making eye contact when you are in conversation is considered proper etiquette in North America. However, keep in mind that in some cultures direct eye contact is considered a breach of etiquette. Asian, Latin American, and Caribbean cultures consider avoiding eye contact to be a sign of respect.

Your Attire

Many countries are much more formal at business meetings than North Americans.

While your company may not have a problem with khakis and golf shirts for business meetings, it is best to wear a traditional suit and tie if you are a man. In most cases a conservative traditional business suit is acceptable for a woman, but there are exceptions. Take time to learn the specifics of women in business in the country of the client, and be considerate of their protocol where reasonable.

Conducting Business

Your company may hold laid-back, casual business meetings, but this doesn't mean your client is comfortable in that setting. Opt for the more formal attitude when you are dealing with foreign clients. Don't be late, and start the business on time. Tardiness can be viewed as an insult.

Also, many cultures do not believe in discussing family or personal issues in a business setting. Keep the business meeting to business and steer clear of personal discussions. Don't assume that anyone will understand your slang or your gestures.

Tips for Traveling

Travelers to foreign countries should try to learn a few phrases in the language of the country you are visiting, as well as the currency system. Also, don't take a picture of a local citizen without first asking permission. Use care when taking pictures of airports, military installations, government buildings and other like buildings, as this is against the law in some countries.

Effective Gift Giving

Bringing a small gift as a token of appreciation seems an appropriate gesture, but take care to learn the gift-giving protocol for the country concerned. Some cultures mandate that gifts be given at the beginning of a business transaction, while other cultures dictate gifts are exchanged at the conclusion of a business deal.

Another consideration is the type of gift you will present. Some countries expect to exchange costly gifts with business associates and others only allow for small token gifts. Color, type, cost and even the wrapping of the gift can all mean different things in different cultures.

For example, in North America white is the color of weddings and black the color of funerals. Be aware that other cultures have different associations with colors you may not be aware of. Did you know that:

- White is the color of mourning in many Asian countries?
- Red is considered good luck in China, but is associated with evil spirits in Central America?
- Yellow has negative connotations in many countries?
- Blue is the color of mourning in some countries?

Wrapping up your gift doesn't seem as if it would be a great challenge, but some cultures consider the presentation (wrapping and giving) of a gift to be as important as the gift itself. The color of the wrapping paper, the type of adornment you choose, and the way the ribbon is tied all can have specific meanings in foreign countries.

> **TIP:** The gift-wrapping rules are very complicated in many Asian countries. If you are entertaining visitors from there, it is often best to ask the hotel concierge where they are staying to handle the wrapping!

3.4.4 Etiquette for Young People

Many parents realize the importance of good manners and proper etiquette for their children, but their fast-paced lifestyles leave them little time to offer this instruction. This opens the door for training opportunities for children and teens. Teaching children is fun and rewarding and teaching the rules of etiquette to children will help them for years to come.

You will find there are many avenues available to offer children and teen etiquette training. You may decide to offer one-on-one training or you may want to teach in small classes or in a workshop. Or you can have a combination for your clients to choose from.

If you decide to take on working with children and teens, you will find yourself working with a group of fun and sometimes funny clients. Make your training fun, too, but keep it informative.

Table manners and telephone etiquette are two of the most requested training classes for children, and you can also offer various communication topics as well.

Table Manners

"Elbows off the table and don't slouch." Almost every mother, at some point or another, has likely spoken these words. With the fast pace of today's lifestyle, it is rare that a family sits down and eats a meal together. This is a loss for the family in time spent bonding, but it is also a lost opportunity to teach table manners to children, who love to imitate.

What is expected of a child is based on their age. You can't expect a two-year-old to sit quietly at the table for 30 minutes, or use the steak knife to cut their chicken. You will use age-appropriate instruction to teach children good table manners:

- Ages 3-6: Children in this age group are still learning the basics. You can encourage holding the spoon or fork correctly and teach children not to use fingers to eat.

- Ages 6-9: A child this age knows how to hold silverware, how to place a napkin in their lap, and how to eat soup without slurping. Also, this is the age where you begin to instill the value of asking for items to be passed and not reaching for them.

- Ages 9-12: Children in this preteen group should have a good grasp of table manners. They may need the occasional reminding, but that is the exception to the rule.

- Ages 13 and up: These children are capable of training for a formal dining experience, as explained in section 2.1.1. The training should still be age-appropriate to hold their interest.

Like adults, teaching children the basics of good table manners is best done in real life settings. In other words, sit down at the table and eat with the children. As an etiquette consultant you can train them in the appropriate behavior, but this behavior must be reinforced in the home to make a lasting impact.

Help the parents by offering a simple set of guidelines that they can adapt for their children. You can include any of the following, and add any areas of concern from the parents as well:

- Come to the table when you are called, or at the appropriate time.

- Wait until everyone is seated until you start eating.

- If saying a blessing over the food is customary, wait for this before eating.

- Don't reach across the table for items. Ask for someone to pass them to you.

- Pass items when requested.

- Use the correct silverware and use it in the appropriate manner.
- Do not talk with your mouth full.
- Take small bites.
- Place your napkin in your lap and use it.
- Wait until everyone is finished before asking to leave the table.
- Thank the person who prepared the meal.

Telephone Etiquette

Telephone manners are a hot button for many adults, and children need to learn early how to properly answer the phone.

How a child answers the phone is the preference of the family. Some families prefer the "Smith residence" while others just like the standard "Hello." Once the greeting is out of the way, children must learn how to respond to the caller. When a caller asks to speak to someone, children should not serve as screeners with a "Who are you?" even if they are curious.

At what age you allow children to answer the phone is a family decision, but many families use writing skills as a benchmark. When the child is old enough to take a message, they are old enough to answer the phone.

Teens present a whole new phone struggle. Many teens monopolize the home phone and disregard calls that are not for them. A teenager might be required to answer the phone and call waiting at all times, and learn to take proper messages for their parents. They might also be expected to respect a time limit on their calls. Many preteens and teens have cellular phones, and can be taught the basics of cell phone etiquette, as explained in section 2.1.5.

Introductions and Greetings

Children need to understand what to say when they are introduced to new people and when they are reintroduced to family friends and relatives. As many children and teens learn best by example and role-playing, reinforcing appropriate introductions and greetings are best done with real-life scenarios. For example, you might invite visitors to a training class and introduce them to each child, or have the children introduce each other to you. When being introduced to someone, children can be taught to:

- Stand up, if seated
- Look at the person who is being introduced
- Smile
- Shake hands
- Say "nice to meet you" or something similar

Along with the appropriate way to meet someone new, children and teens need to learn how to introduce friends to others. This can start with children introducing friends to parents. For example: "Mom, this is Johnny Mitchell. He just moved in next door." Parents can reinforce this training by finding opportunities for their children to use their introduction skills.

Older children and teens can take the introductions a step further and include a brief statement when they are greeting or introducing people. For example: "Hello, Mr. Smith. I'm Julie Moore and I go to school with your daughter," or, "Mr. Smith, I would like you to meet my Mother, Mary Moore. She teaches English at XYZ Academy."

Another etiquette stumbling block for many families is how children should address adults. Within the family, children should call older family members by their title and given name (e.g. Uncle Eric). A child, even a teen, should never address a parent by a given name.

Conversation and Listening Skills

Children were once taught that they were to be seen and not heard. This is no longer the case, but children do need to understand when it is appropriate for them to join in an adult conversation. Conversational skills can be taught in a role-playing setting, using children attending your training and volunteer adults. Here are some conversational and listening tips for children:

- Do not interrupt anyone speaking.

- Respond when someone asks you a direct question.
- Don't mumble.
- Look at the person speaking.
- Don't finish someone else's story (adults are prone to this too).
- Don't leave the room when someone is speaking, unless it is an emergency.
- Pay attention to the conversation at hand.

3.4.5 Wedding Etiquette

This section outlines some of the common areas of concern your clients may have regarding wedding etiquette. From announcing the engagement to seating the parents, couples are bound to have questions about etiquette throughout the process of planning their wedding.

In the world of wedding etiquette, there are some absolute musts, such as handwritten thank-you notes, and some traditions that are no longer required, such as the bride's family paying the bulk of the expenses.

Who Pays for What

It's important to establish a budget for your wedding upfront. There is a traditional breakdown of who pays for what, but keep in mind that these are not requirements. You, your fiancé, and your families may decide another way to distribute the expenses. It is necessary to clearly communicate with each other when determining the financial responsibilities, to prevent any surprises after the wedding arrangements are underway.

The following is a list of the traditional guidelines that you can use as a starting point for discussions and planning.

The Bride and Bride's Family Pay For

- Groom's wedding ring and wedding gift
- Groom's boutonniere
- Gifts for the bridesmaids
- All stationery, such as announcements, invitations, programs, thank-you cards
- Wedding gown and accessories
- Bridesmaids' bouquets
- Ceremony, including flowers, accessories like arches, and any church and musician fees
- Reception, including food and servers, cake, flowers, and wedding favors
- Photography and videography
- Band or DJ
- Transportation of wedding party from ceremony to reception

The Groom and Groom's Family Pay For

- Bride's wedding ring and wedding gift
- Bride's bouquet
- Gifts for the groomsmen and ushers
- Marriage license
- Rehearsal dinner
- Mothers' and grandmothers' corsages
- Boutonnieres for the groomsmen and the ushers
- Officiant fee
- Groom's cake
- Transportation of bride and groom after reception
- Honeymoon arrangements

Each attendant pays for his or her own attire. Each guest pays their own travel expenses, though you should help by reserving blocks of rooms in nearby hotels.

Invitations

You, your fiancé, your parents, and his parents should make a list of everyone you want to invite. If the number of people is too many, you will all need to make some cuts from the list, which can be difficult. It is polite to try to keep the number of invitations balanced on both your side and the groom's side.

Traditionally, the bride's parents host the wedding, which is reflected in the invitation wording. However, you can word the invitations in a variety of ways.

When addressing invitations, you can convey whether guests or children are invited, but you should never write "no guest" or "no children." If a single guest is welcome to bring a companion, write "add guest" on the inner envelope. If a guest is welcome to bring their children, write the childrens' names on the inner envelope.

Include an RSVP card so you can get an accurate count of how many people are coming. Consider that, on average, about 25 percent of the invited guests may not make it. You can also keep a secondary list of people to invite, and as the people on your primary list return their cards, send additional invitations to people on the secondary list as space becomes available.

It is common to send invitations about eight weeks prior to the wedding to give guests time to make arrangements to attend. Include a card containing information about hotel accommodations in invitations to out-of-town guests. It is also increasingly common to send "Save the Date" cards between six and nine months before the wedding, stating the wedding date and including hotel information.

Asking for Gifts

Registering for gifts for your home as a married couple can be fun, but try not to appear too materialistic when publicizing this information. The most tactful way to let people know where you are registered is by word of mouth. You should never mention gift registries on the wedding invitation. However, it is now commonly acceptable to list registries on shower invitations. You can also set up a wedding website to share information about your upcoming wedding with friends and family, and list your gift registries there. The Knot is a good place to get started if you want to set up a wedding website. You can find them at **www.theknot.com**.

If you would prefer cash gifts or gift certificates, you should rely on word of mouth for this. But realize that some people may not want to give cash gifts, for example, because it may feel impersonal to them. There is also a new trend of setting up honeymoon registries, where guests can contribute money towards your honeymoon expenses. Examples include: *The Big Day* at **www.thebigday.com**, as well as *HoneyLuna*, found at **www.honeyluna.com**.

If this is not your first marriage, know that gifts are not mandatory. However, unless you specify otherwise, etiquette suggests that guests give gifts such as gift certificates to restaurants and spas. For a good resource for etiquette regarding second weddings, see **www.idotaketwo.com**.

For any gifts that you receive, keep in mind that it is improper to use any of the gifts until after the wedding.

Showers

Your honor attendant or other friends may host your bridal shower. Traditionally, unless an immediate family member is an honor attendant, an immediate family member should not host a shower for you.

You can have multiple showers, and coed showers for both you and your fiancé are also popular. Guests can be invited to more than one shower, but they are not expected to buy more than one shower gift.

All wedding guests do not need to be invited to a shower, but if someone is invited to a shower they should also be invited to your wedding. The only exception is office showers given at your workplace.

Seating Family at the Wedding

When seating parents for the ceremony, your parents sit in the front pew on the left, while the groom's parents sit in the front pew on the right. If a parent is widowed, it is fine for a guest to sit up front with them.

Seating arrangements can get more complicated if parents are divorced. The mother should sit in the front pew, with her husband if she is remarried. The mother's immediate family sits in the second row, and third row too if necessary. The father should sit in the next row back, with his wife if he is remarried, and their family members. This standard applies to both your side and the groom's side.

However, this can get more complicated if the divorced parents are not friendly with each other, and especially if there is anger among family members. For example, if your mother is angry towards your father's new wife, it would be nicer of the new spouse to sit further back with other people.

And other configurations may be necessary. For example, if your parents are divorced, but you grew up with your father and stepmother, you can change the seating arrangements to sit your father and stepmother in the front pew. Or, if the divorced parents are very friendly, all parents and stepparents can sit on the front pew together. If you do have a situation with family tensions, it is important to work through the seating arrangements before the wedding and communicate the seating arrangements to the family members, to avoid any confusion or mishaps at the wedding.

Toasts

The father of the bride, with a toast, makes engagement announcements. Wedding toasts are offered to the bride and groom beginning with the best man. The groom often responds with a toast of thanks. Other toasts may be offered in the following order: Fathers, beginning with the father of the bride; Mothers, beginning with the mother of the bride; Groom to the bride; and Bride to the groom.

Postponed or Cancelled Weddings

If a wedding is postponed for some reason (such as a family illness) or cancelled altogether, you should let your guests know as soon as possible. It is proper to provide an explanation for a postponement, but not for a cancellation. Any gifts received should be returned if the wedding is cancelled or the marriage is annulled.

Thank-You Notes

Thank-you notes should be personal and always handwritten. Each gift you receive should be acknowledged with its own thank-you note, for example, if someone gives you both a shower gift and a wedding gift, you should write separate thank-you notes for each gift.

Sample Thank-You Note

Dear Robert and Jan,

Thank you so much for the crystal wine glasses. We now have a complete set! Adam and I are looking forward to your next visit, when we can enjoy a drink together. Thank you again for thinking of us at this special time in our lives.

Much love,
Sarah

Rules on when you should send thank-you notes vary. For shower gifts and wedding gifts that arrive before the wedding, advice ranges from acknowledging them as soon as possible to within no more than two weeks. For gifts received at the wedding, advice ranges from acknowledging them within two weeks to no more than eight weeks after the honeymoon.

In a thank-you note, mention the gift positively and state how you plan to use it. This also applies to cash gifts. The tone of the thank-you note should be warm and sincere, such as in this example:

Additional Resources

Wedding etiquette is a vast area of knowledge, and there is a wealth of resources available to help with wedding etiquette questions or concerns that you have. Some examples of websites you may find useful include:

- *OurMarriage.com: Wedding Etiquette*
  www.ourmarriage.com/html/wedding_etiquette.html

- *Wedding Etiquette Advice*
  www.topweddingsites.com/wedding_etiquette.html

- *iVillage: Articles on Wedding Etiquette*
  http://love.ivillage.com
  (Scroll over “Love & Marriage”, then choose “Weddings” from the pop-up menu. Click on “Etiquette Essentials”)

- *Peggy Post’s World of Wedding Etiquette*
  http://wedding.weddingchannel.com/invitations/wedding_etiquette.asp

- *The Knot: Etiquette*
  www.theknot.com/keywords/sc_148_527.shtml

4. Starting Your Own Etiquette Consulting Business

> *"Etiquette consulting is a business which grows beautifully with time and patience."*
>
> – Pamela Bedour, The Protocol School of Ontario

If being your own boss appeals to you, the good news is that starting an etiquette consulting business can be done without investing a large amount of money. You can start small, or even part time, and grow your business to a level you are comfortable with.

4.1 Getting Started

If you have an entrepreneurial background you will hit the ground running. If not, this section will walk you through the process of starting a consulting business, with resources for further study.

4.1.1 Small Business Resources

You are not alone as you get ready to start your own business. There are many resources you can call on for help. These are among the best:

- *Small Business Administration*
  This organization offers help with business start-ups and has a variety of programs and services for the small business owner. There is at least one SBA office in every state in the United States. Call the Answer Desk at 1-800-U-ASK-SBA (827-5722) or visit:
  www.sbaonline.sba.gov

- *SCORE*
  This organization has over 10,000 volunteers who provide counseling and mentoring to new business start-ups. They also offer business tips on their website. Call 1-800-634-0245 or visit:
  www.score.org

- *Canadian Business Service Centres*
  You will find a wide range of information at this site, including a step-by-step guide to walk you through starting your new business.
  www.cbsc.org/osbw

- *Nolo.com*
  Nolo is a publisher of plain English legal information. Their website also offers free advice on a variety of other small business matters. At their website click on the "Business & Human Resources" tab, then on "Starting a Business."
  www.nolo.com

Now, let's take a look at the first thing you need to do to get started: creating a business plan.

4.1.2 Create a Business Plan

If you think that business plans are only for those big mega companies, think again. A business plan doesn't have to be a confusing document written in a language only a lawyer can understand. A business plan is just that… your plan to do business.

There are some good business plan models available to use as guides. Many entrepreneurs use the United States Small Business Administration's (SBA's) business plan outline as a model. The Canada Business Service Centres (CBSC) also provides a sample business plan at their website. Small Business Lending Corporation has developed an online business plan workshop to take you through writing a business plan step by step.

- *SBA: Business Plan Basics*
  www.sba.gov/starting_business/planning/basic.html

- *CBSC: Business Start-Up Assistant*
  http://bsa.cbsc.org

- *Small Business Lending Corporation*
  www.smallbizlending.com/resources/workshop/main.asp

Creating a business plan makes you think about what you want your business to be and how you plan to make it happen. A business plan answers the following questions:

- What services will you provide?
- Who are your competitors and what makes you different and better?
- Who will be your customers? How will you reach these customers?
- How will you market your business?
- How much will you charge for your services?
- How much money will you need to get started? Where will you get the money?

The main body of your business plan will be divided into the four sections listed below:

- A description of your business
- Your marketing plan
- Your financial management plan
- Your management plan

In addition to those parts, your plan should include the following extra material and information:

- An executive summary
- Supporting documents
- Financial projections
- A cover sheet
- A statement of purpose
- A table of contents

If the prospect of writing a business plan sounds daunting or confusing, hang in there. We'll take a closer look at each of these parts.

Description of Your Business

A description of your business is just that — a description of the business you plan to start and run. The trick is to include the unique and special things about your business so that everyone who reads your business plan will know you're on to something really fabulous.

You'll need to state in this section that, as a consultant, you'll be operating a service business. Get specific about the services you'll provide. If you will specialize in executive coaching and business etiquette, for instance, state that in your description. The idea is to paint a picture of the business you plan to start.

You should also explain what the legal structure of your business will be. Will you have a sole proprietorship, for instance, or perhaps a partnership? You'll learn more about legal structures a little later in this section of the chapter.

Also in this section, you'll need to explain why your business will be profitable, and how your consulting business will be different and better than any others in the area. What do you plan to offer that will have clients beating down your doors, begging you to be their consultant?

TIP: When writing your business plan, pay close attention to spelling and grammar, and try to write clearly and concisely. You don't want to make reading the plan a chore.

Describe your business hours. As a consultant, you'll most likely need to have flexible hours to accommodate the schedules of your clients. But if you plan only to work from 10:00 a.m. until 2:00 p.m. three days a week, you should make that clear. Also, you should identify the planned location of your business, the type of space you'll have, and why it's conducive to your business.

Conclude the description of your business by clearly identifying your goals and objectives and supporting them with information and knowledge you've acquired about being a consultant. This is important, because it's here that you're explaining exactly why you're starting this business and what you hope to accomplish with it.

Your Marketing Plan

How well you market your business has a lot to do with the degree of success you'll experience. The most important elements of a good marketing plan are defining your market and knowing your customers. Knowing your customers is important because it allows you to identify their likes and dislikes and tailor your services to accommodate them.

You don't want to limit yourself to a very narrow market, because that can affect your chances of getting funding, as well as limit the scope of your business once it's underway. So if you're going to specialize in executive coaching and business etiquette, your market should be the entire corporate community, not just one area of it. Your marketing plan should paint a picture of a wide and ready market, just waiting for your consulting services. Your marketing plan also must address the areas listed below:

Competition

Businesses compete for customers, market share, publicity and so forth. It's smart to know who your competitors are and exactly what they're doing. In order to provide services that are different and better, you need to look carefully at your competitors' products and services, how they're promoting them, and who's buying them.

Pricing

You'll learn more about setting fees later in this chapter, but know that you should address it, at least briefly, in your business plan. This section should consider factors such as competitive pricing, costs of labor and materials, overhead and so forth.

Advertising and Public Relations

You need to think about how you'll advertise your business, making sure that whatever means of advertising you choose accurately portrays the image you want to convey. The next chapter has many ideas for marketing your business.

Your Financial Management Plan

Financial management is crucial to running a successful business. Your business plan should describe both your startup costs and your operating costs.

The startup budget includes all the costs necessary to get your business up and running. Operating costs are ongoing expenses, such as advertising, utilities, rent and so forth.

Remember to include the following items in your budgets. Notice that some expenses overlap on the startup and operating budgets.

- **Startup budget:** Legal and professional fees, licenses and permits, equipment, insurance, supplies, advertising and promotions, accounting expenses, utilities, payroll expenses.

- **Operating budget:** Make a budget for your first three to six months of operation, including expenses such as: personnel (even if it's only your own salary), insurance, rent, loan payments, advertising and promotions, legal and accounting fees, supplies, utilities, dues and subscriptions, fees, taxes and maintenance.

Your financial management plan also should address the accounting system you plan to use. Many small business owners conduct their own accounting, using software such as QuickBooks, while others hire someone to set up a system. You can find the Quickbooks website at **www.quickbooks.intuit.com**.

Your Management Plan

Managing a business, no matter how big or small or it is, requires organization and discipline. Your management plan should be carefully thought out, well-written, and should address issues such as:

- Your background and business experience, and how they'll be beneficial to your consulting business.
- The members of your management team (even if you'll be the only member).
- Assistance you expect to receive (this can be financial help, consulting and advice or whatever).
- The duties for which you and any employee or employees will be responsible.
- Plans for hiring employees, either now or in the future.
- A general overview of how your business will be run.

In addition to these major areas, your business plan should include the extras mentioned earlier:

- **A cover sheet.** This identifies your business and explains the purpose of the business plan. Be sure to include your name, the name of the business and the name of any partners, if applicable; your address, phone number, email address and other pertinent information.
- **Table of contents.** This goes just under your cover sheet and tells what's included in your business plan. Use major headings and subheadings to identify the contents.
- **Statement of purpose.** This is important because it summarizes your goals and objectives. A statement of purpose should sum up your hopes and dreams.
- **Executive summary.** Basically, this is a thumbnail sketch of your business plan. It should summarize everything you've included in the main body of the plan.

- **Financial projections.** This is an idea of how much money you'll need to start your business, and how much you expect to earn. Remember to support your projections with explanations.

- **Supporting documents.** Include your personal (and business, if applicable) tax returns for the past three years, a personal financial statement (get a form from your bank) and a copy of a lease or purchase agreement if you will buy or rent office space.

A good business plan will require some time and work on your part, but it's really essential to getting your business off on the right track. If you make the effort to draw up a good plan now, you can be confident that it will pay off in the future.

4.1.3 Selecting the Right Business Name

In the etiquette consulting business, you want to have a business name that identifies your services but doesn't limit your growth. If you only plan to offer dining etiquette and name your business Dining Manners or Table Manners, then it will be difficult for you to market your services if you decide later to offer international protocol training.

Most etiquette consultants use easily identifiable names, and don't try to make the name too cutesy or funny. Also, stay away from hard to spell or pronounce words or words with unclear meanings. When you consider names, think about:

- Your target customers

- The benefits you will bring to your customers

- Words or phrases that appeal to your customers

- The names of your competitors

Sit down and brainstorm name ideas. Try to come up with eight to ten names, and then put them aside. Call on five or six close friends and family members whose judgment you trust and ask for their input. To get you thinking creatively, here are a few names of existing etiquette consulting businesses. As you'll see below, you can't use business names owned by someone else, but doing an informal Internet search can help you identify what types of names you like best.

- A Charming Experience
- Courtesy Counts
- Correctitudes
- Executive Protocol Group
- Etiquette Ladies
- Polished Professionals
- The Right Fork

If you plan to do business under a name other than your own personal name, you may need to file your business name with your local government. Filing an assumed or fictitious name (also known as a "DBA", which is short for "doing business as") is a simple process that involves filling out a short form and paying a small fee to your local, state, or provincial government office.

Before officially registering your business name, you must conduct formal fictitious names and trademark searches. (The fictitious names database is where non-trademarked business names are listed.) One good free resource for this type of search is the Thomas Register at **www.thomasnet.com**.

A trademark database lists all registered and trademarked business names. In the U.S., the essential place to start is with the U.S. Patent and Trademark Office. You can hire a company to do a name search for you, or conduct a free search yourself at **www.uspto.gov/main/trademarks.htm**. In Canada, the default database for name searches is Newly Upgraded Automated Name Search (NUANS) at **www.nuans.com**. There is a $20 charge for each NUANS search.

> **TIP:** Registering your business name is not a necessity for small businesses, but it will prevent others from using your name. It is a requirement, however, if you are incorporating.

Addtional advice on naming your business can be found at **www.nolo.com**. Choose "Starting a Business" under the "Business & Human Resources" tab, then click on "Naming Your Business."

4.1.4 Your Business Structure

How your business is structured will have an impact on your startup costs, taxes, and liability. When you set out to develop your business structure, you may want to work with an attorney to ensure you handle all the appropriate legal paperwork.

Following are the pros and cons of several different legal forms a business can take, although you will most likely choose a sole proprietorship, at least to begin. You should keep the other structures in mind as you grow your business. You can find out more about business structures at the links mentioned in section 4.1.1.

Sole Proprietorship

Many new businesses start out as sole proprietorships because it is an easy and inexpensive way to organize your business.

Pros

- Easy to start, no special documents or forms needed (other than the fictitious name or DBA filing).
- As the owner, you have complete control of the business.
- Not treated as a separate taxable entity.

Cons

- As the owner you hold all responsibility and liability for the business.
- You can't bring on a partner in a sole proprietorship.
- You might have difficulty convincing investors that they should give their money to you.

Partnerships

A partnership structure allows two or more people to work together as co-owners of the business. A partnership agreement is a document that is essential in all partnerships. Before you go into business with anyone, even your best friend, you need to know exactly what is expected of you, and your partner needs to know what you expect.

Spend some time discussing just what your individual duties will be, including how much money will each of you invest in the business startup, which areas of the business will each of you be responsible for, whether your percentages of ownership will be equal (50-50), and what the plans are for the future.

Pros

- More than one owner helps to share the workload.
- Simple to form and easy to operate.

Cons

- Partners are liable for each other's actions, not just their own.
- Can be viewed to have a lack of stability; the partnership dissolves if one partner dies or withdraws.
- Possible difficulty raising capital.

Corporations

If you want to limit your personal liability and make your business appear more professional, you may want to incorporate your business. A corporation is a legal business entity that is separate from the individuals who own it. Incorporating your business doesn't come cheap. And along with that price tag come rules and regulations, including filing articles of incorporation, holding regular meetings of the corporation officers, and keeping a record of the minutes from all meetings.

Pros

- Limited liability. As a rule of thumb, the shareholders (you and your partners, if you have any) aren't responsible for the debts and obligations of the corporation.
- Appears more professional.
- Easier to raise capital.

Cons

- Expensive to form and maintain.
- Complicated paperwork to file.

- Must pay corporate taxes, along with personal taxes on any salary you pay yourself.

Limited Liability Companies (LLCs)

This relatively new (U.S.-only) business structure combines the best of corporations with the best of partnerships. Many small- to mid-sized businesses are now choosing the LLC structure.

Pros

- Members of the LLC are shielded from personal liability.
- Pay no corporate taxes.
- Can have multiple members.

Cons

- Many jurisdictions don't allow LLCs to have only one member.
- Costs more to form and maintain than a sole proprietorship.

4.1.5 Insurance

You work hard to create a solid and reputable business, so consider insurance policies to make certain that your investment isn't wiped out by some unseen circumstance or disaster. Types of insurance for the small business owner include the following. Contact an insurance broker to find out what types of coverage are right for you.

- **Liability Insurance:** This policy will protect you if you are sued. It will pay judgments against you (up to the policy limits) along with any legal fees you incur defending yourself.

- **Property Insurance:** This insurance covers losses to your personal property from damage or theft. If you run a home office. you want to have the contents of your business listed on the policy, or have a separate policy if you rent office space.

- **Business Interruption Insurance:** This insurance covers your bills and lost profit while you are out of operation for a covered loss, such as a fire. Just because the business is shut down doesn't mean the bills stop coming.

- **Health Insurance:** If you aren't covered under a spouse's health plan, you'll need to consider your health insurance options. You can check with local membership organizations, such as the Chamber of Commerce or national organizations for health insurance options for their members. Individual insurance is often expensive, but some insurance companies offer discount pricing for members of specific organizations.

- **Life and Disability Insurance:** If you provide a portion of your family's income, then you need to carry life insurance and disability insurance to make certain they are cared for if something happens to you.

4.2 Financial Matters

The good news is that as an etiquette consultant, you may not have to wait too long to earn your first dollar. You can make it through that first lean year with some careful planning and budgeting, and smart purchases. In this section we'll take a look at money matters, such as:

- Getting funding for your first year
- Setting up a budget that is manageable
- Paying business taxes
- Setting your fees properly for a profit

4.2.1 Start-Up Funding

As long as you have access to a telephone and a computer, an etiquette consulting business can be started for next to nothing, and you can even work it part time and keep your regular job until the business starts earning significant money.

If you are going into this business as your full-time job, the rule of thumb is to have at least six months of living expenses, beyond your startup capital, banked before you start a business with no other income coming in. This gives you the time to build up your business and start earning some money for when your nest egg runs out.

So, if you decide to produce professionally printed promotional materials and buy advertising, and figure that you need $5,000 to get your business up and running, and $1,000 a month to keep it operating smoothly, you should try to have between $10,000 and $12,000 available in advance. If you plan to take etiquette consulting training, you will want to have a few thousand dollars set aside for that as well (see section 2.3.1 for programs and fees).

Funding Sources

If you're wondering where you're going to come up with that much money, consider these possible sources:

Your Personal Savings

This includes bank accounts, 401(k) funds or other retirement savings, mutual funds, money market accounts and stock accounts. Just be sure that you don't spend so much of your personal money that you can't meet your personal expenses.

Credit Cards and Lines of Credit

These are great vehicles for "stop-gap money" — that is, money you need right away to pay for something that you know money is coming in for, such as printing materials for a workshop. But try not to use credit on a long-term basis. You'll end up paying costly interest that can really drag down your business.

Collateral

A lender often will agree to loan you money if they are assured they'll get something of value in the event that you default on the loan. A business just starting up can't count as collateral, so you'll probably need to put up personal assets like your house or your car. It's a guarantee to the lender that they'll get the money, and the interest on it, back.

Private Placement Firms

Sometimes called "money finders," these firms will try to get money from business investors on your behalf. Of course, they don't perform this service for nothing. They usually take a percentage of the money they find for you, or you have to agree to pay them a percentage of your profits.

Family and Friends

Borrowing from family and friends can be tricky, but if you know someone who has money and is willing to loan it to you, it might be worth considering. Just make sure you have a legal agreement that outlines repayment terms and so forth. And make it clear that the loan doesn't give the family member a right to tell you how to run your business.

Lending Institutions

These include traditional banks, credit unions, savings and loans and commercial finance companies. Be sure to compare interest rates and terms of lending to see which institution offers the best deals. Be prepared to write a proposal outlining why the bank should lend you money, how you plan to repay it, and why your consulting business is going to be the best.

4.2.2 Budgeting

Whether you fund your startup with personal savings, loans from family or a loan from your bank, you need to have a good idea where the money is needed and where it is going. Many businesses fail because they don't put a budget in place and have no idea how much they are spending until it is too late.

> **TIP:** If you don't want to pay for every service you need, consider bartering, or trading your service for theirs. Bartering can be very helpful when you are starting out in business and you have more time than cash flow. For example, you could do a workshop for five employees in return for 1000 brochures. You may also want to join a bartering group and then when you need a good or service, you can get it through the barter group. Many areas have local bartering groups, so check your Yellow Pages or with your local Chamber of Commerce.

Sample Monthly Budget

Creating your budget gives you an idea of what to expect your first year. You can then use the budgeted numbers and the actual numbers to build a budget for year two. Your monthly budget will also help you determine what costs you need to cover before you start making a profit.

Following is a sample budget for you to review. (Your numbers will be different.) Fill in your numbers in the blanks provided to determine your monthly budget.

	Sample	Yours
Rent	$ 100	_________
Telephone	120	_________
Internet service provider cost	75	_________
Postage	35	_________
Office supplies	75	_________
Travel expenses	75	_________
Business insurance	25	_________
Taxes	100	_________
Club/Organization dues	20	_________
Marketing and advertising costs	200	_________
Magazine subscriptions	10	_________
Business checking account	15	_________
Accounting costs	150	_________
Total	$1,000 /month	_________

Startup Cost Checklist

Use the following list to get an idea of what your business start up will cost you and what the monthly cost will be after start up. Note that just because an item is on the list, doesn't mean you have to budget for it. You may not need it, or you may already have it. You should also consider if there are expenses not on this list that will apply to you.

Possible Start-Up Costs

_________ Office furniture

_________ Computer

_________ Printer

_________ Fax machine

_________ Office software

_________ Business phone line installation fee

_________ Telephone

_________ Office supplies

_________ Stationery

_________ Business cards

_________ Printing (brochures, flyers or other marketing materials)

_________ Website setup costs (design, domain name, etc.)

_________ Business licenses/fees

_________ Professional consulting (lawyer, accountant)

_________ Initial etiquette training

Possible Monthly Overhead Costs

_________ Rent (or portion of mortgage)

_________ Telephone bill (two lines and toll-free number)

_________ Internet service bill

_________ Web hosting

_________ Postage (for mailing brochures, proposals, etc.)

_________ Office supplies

_________ Travel expenses (mileage and overnight expenses)

_________ Insurance costs

_________ Taxes (this is payroll, if necessary, or self-employment tax and other business tax. Your figures can vary greatly depending on the legal structure of your business)

_________ Club/organization dues

_________ Marketing and advertising expenses (your brochures, business marketing materials, ad space you purchase, and other ad costs)

_________ Magazine subscriptions and professional literature

_________ Business checking account

_________ Printing handouts

_________ Ongoing training/conferences

_________ Legal and accounting services (if you decide to have a professional handle your books, this cost will vary depending on how much the accountant does and the average costs in your area)

4.2.3 Taxes

No one likes to think about paying taxes, but starting a new business without considering the tax situation is like bungee jumping without the cord. You need to understand how your new business will be taxed, and when those taxes must be paid.

Your new business will be responsible for paying taxes when you start making money, but it's a good idea to have all your paperwork in place before you earn your first dollar.

If you are operating your business as a sole proprietorship in the United States, then you will need to file a Schedule C with your individual income tax return. You may also be required to pay quarterly estimated payments for your income and self-employment taxes.

If you are a corporation, partnership or LLC, you will need to file for an EIN (employer identification number) before you file taxes. In fact, some sole proprietors chose to have an EIN instead of using their Social Security Number as their business identification number. To receive an EIN you need to file an SS-4 Application for Employer Identification Number. You can find this form at: *Internal Revenue Service: SS-4 Application for EIN*, **www.irs.gov/pub/irs-pdf/fss4.pdf**.

If your company is a corporation, partnership or LLC, you will also need to file specific forms based on the structure of your business. For more information on taxes, visit these sites:

- *Nolo*
  (Click the "Business & Human Resources" tab, then "Making a Profit", then "Saving Business Taxes")
  www.nolo.com

- *IRS Tax Information for Businesses*
  www.irs.ustreas.gov/businesses

- *Canadian Small Business & Self Employed Tax Information*
  www.cra-arc.gc.ca/tax/business

4.2.4 Setting Your Fees

There are a number of ways that etiquette consultants set fees. They may use one of the following, or a combination of:

- An hourly fee
- A daily fee
- A per-person fee (based on number of people to train)
- A per-project or per-service basis

However you choose to set your fees, they should include an hourly rate for your consulting service, any materials you supply, travel to and from the seminar, and rental of presentation space. They should also cover a portion of your overhead that month.

Another consideration in setting fees for a specific project is how much preparation time is involved. If you are being asked to custom-design a program for a company, you will have to factor in the time it will take you to prepare the presentation. However, if you are being hired to do a general presentation on cell phone etiquette, your prep time will be much shorter.

When you calculate your hourly consultation rate, remember that as a consultant, you may only work a few billable days a week, and your fees will have to be high enough so that you can make a living. Refer back to your monthly budget for these numbers. Once you have a budget in place, you have to decide just how much you want to earn. Be realistic and know that your income will grow each year. Knowing how much you want to earn helps you as you set your fees, market your business, and plan for the years to come.

For example, a new etiquette consultant might have a first-year goal of $30,000 of income after expenses. If they will have $10,000 of expenses, they will need to earn $40,000 to meet their goal. Charging $100 an hour will mean that they need to bill 400 hours in the year. Considering that there are 52 weeks in a year, they should be spending about 8 hours a week with paying clients.

Following are a variety of options for setting your fees. When setting your own fees remember that you don't want to overprice yourself, but you also don't want to sell yourself short. Undercutting your competition will not benefit you in the long run. Price implies value to some people and if you price your services below everyone else in town, people will wonder why you are so cheap.

If you find your fees are way out of line with the competition, you should go back and look at how you arrived at your numbers. You may be trying to be too profitable too quickly, or you may have expenses that could be cut.

Hourly Fees

An hourly rate is a common way for etiquette consultants to set their fees, particularly when they are working one-on-one with a client. Remember that this is a consulting fee, and additional expenses are extra. Hourly fees will apply to any initial consultations with the client, and the time it takes you to customize programs to suit a particular purpose, or you may develop a flat rate for these services.

For the beginning etiquette consultant, an average hourly fee is between $40 and $60 an hour, depending on the demand for service and the geographical area. For etiquette consultants with a bit of experience, $100 an hour or more is normal, and $200 an hour is not an uncommon price in the major metropolitan areas such as Los Angeles and New York. Phyllis Davis, a top etiquette trainer with 30 years of expertise, told us she charges $500 an hour for one-on-one consultation.

> **TIP:** An established consultant will likely increase rates by about 15 percent each year. Given this increase, a new consultant starting out at $50 an hour will double their hourly rate in just five years.

Daily Fees

Fees for corporate training programs are typically charged by the day. Fees vary, but it is not unusual to charge several thousand dollars a day for a training program. However, if an organization has a specific amount budgeted, and it's a topic you specialize in (meaning you won't have to do a lot of extra research), you might decide to be flexible on the fee. Phyllis Davis, the same top trainer with 30 years experience mentioned earlier, charges $10,000 a day for corporate training.

The *FabJob Guide to Become a Motivational Speaker* says that when you are starting out, you may find that the organizations that ask you to speak will tell you what they are offering to pay. For example, if an organization only has a speaker budget of a few hundred dollars, they will usually say so up front.

However, these are the exceptions to the rule. As a professional speaker or trainer, you are the one who decides what your fees will be. Many employers will ask "What are your fees?" when you discuss working together. If you are asked this question you need to have an answer.

If you don't have an answer, or say "it's negotiable," you will not sound like a professional. Professional speakers and trainers have "fee schedules" that they provide on request to prospective clients (although some trainers are willing to negotiate their published fees).

Sample Fee Schedule

Keynote (up to 90 minutes):	$1,000
Half day seminar (up to 3 hours):	$1,500
Full day seminar (up to 6 hours):	$2,000

Outside of *(your city)* add airfare, hotel, and expenses.

A fee schedule is a published list of fees for different lengths of speaking engagements. Most speakers and trainers have a fee for a keynote presentation (up to 90 minutes in length), a half-day presentation, and a full day presentation, as shown in the sample above.

A beginner who speaks to schools might start at $200 and raise the price as they get more bookings. On the other hand, a beginner with professional materials who is booked to speak at conferences might start at $1,000 per keynote.

Charging by the Person

Creating a fee per person for a seminar or workshop is another common way that etiquette consultants charge. To set your consulting fee for a group, you can charge your hourly one-on-one consulting rate for every two people (i.e., half your hourly rate, per person).

For example, if your usual fee is $100 an hour to consult in person, and there are 30 people attending, your fee for the presentation would be $50 times 30 people, or $1,500 an hour, plus any additional expenses.

Project-Based Fees

When you deal with large organizations and corporations they will want fees based on a project. What that project involves will likely be different for each client. For example, say a company wants you to present the following four programs:

1. Communication workshop customized for the 12-person customer service department

2. Communication workshop customized for the 30-person sales force

3. Business etiquette for the 11-person management staff

4. One-on-one training for three executives

You could calculate your fees as shown in the sample below, based on your $100 an hour one-on-one rate.

Sample Project-Based Fee

2-hour communication workshop for 12 customer service employees

$50 per person times 12 people	=	$600 per hour
$600 times two hours	=	$1,200
Add $10 per person for materials	+	$120
TOTAL	=	$1,320

2-hour communication workshop for 30 sales people

$50 per person times 30 people	=	$1,500 per hour

If you decide to offer this in two sessions to more manageable groups of 15

$1,500 times two hours	=	$3,000
Add $10 per person for materials	+	$300
TOTAL	=	$3,300

2-hour business etiquette presentation for 11 managers

$50 per person times 11 people	=	$550 per hour
$550 times two hours	=	$1,100
Add $6 per person for materials	+	$66
TOTAL	=	$1,166

Three hours each one-on-one training for three executives		
$100 per person times three people	=	$300 per hour
$300 times three hours	=	$900
TOTAL	=	$900
TOTAL PROJECT PRICE	=	**$6,686**

Your final quote to the organization could also include your travel expenses and initial consultation fees. For example, you might charge $500 for an initial consultation.

4.3 Your Place of Business

Once you hammer out all the business startup issues, it's time to get your business set up. In this section we will look at location options for your business, and the small list of equipment and supplies you will need.

4.3.1 Location

Where will you house your new business? Many etiquette consultants start their businesses in a home office and later move them out of their homes, while others choose to keep their office in their home for the long term.

Before you can decide where you want to house your business, you have to determine what functions you need your office to serve. Consider the services you provide and what tasks you will need to do in your office.

Consider whether you will meet with clients at your office. Many etiquette consultants don't, and always travel to the client's home or place of business. You will also need to consider if you have enough space to store your materials, and space for future (or current) employees to work.

Home Office

This is the cheapest and easiest office location. And don't forget the short commute time. If you have the space in your home to set up a dedicated office that will allow you to run your business, then you may want to consider this option.

You'll need to check your local zoning laws, as some areas don't allow you to run a business from your home, while others have no such restrictions. There are other areas that allow you to run a business as long as no clients come to your home. Make sure that you know your zoning laws before you proceed.

Working from your home offers the additional benefits of easier setup, claiming a home office deduction on your taxes (if you meet the criteria), and generally more time with family. Cons include the inevitable distraction from family and neighbors, working too much, failing to separate work and personal life, feeling isolated, and lack of space.

Leasing Office Space

If working from home is not possible, then you need to rent office space. Here is a checklist to review as you consider each potential office space:

Office Space Checklist

- ☐ Will this be an **easy commute** for me? (You don't want to have to battle traffic to and from work every day if you can avoid it.)
- ☐ Is the neighborhood or district **safe**? (You want to feel comfortable in your office and you want this for your employees also.)
- ☐ Is the parking area **lit well**? (Drive by the area at night and look at the lighting. Man or woman, you don't want to have to walk to your car in the dark.)
- ☐ Is the parking **convenient** for my employees, my clients, and me? (You don't want to lug your stuff across a long parking lot and neither does anyone else.)
- ☐ Is there space for **growth**? (You don't want to have to move to a bigger office next year.)
- ☐ Can I **afford** it? (You'll want to read your lease agreement carefully, and crunch some numbers in your budget before you agree.)

4.3.2 Equipment and Supplies

Once you get your office location nailed down, you have to outfit your office. You need a comfortable and well-lit workspace, and somewhere to store your records, supplies, and materials. The specific equipment and supplies you choose will depend on your personal taste and décor, but here is an overview you can examine.

Equipment and Supplies Checklist

Supplies and Small Equipment

- ☐ Accordion files
- ☐ Binders
- ☐ Business cards
- ☐ Business stationery
- ☐ Calculator
- ☐ Calendar or calendar software
- ☐ File folders
- ☐ File labels
- ☐ Flip chart
- ☐ Index cards
- ☐ Laser pointer (to use with presentations)
- ☐ Mailing labels
- ☐ Mailing envelopes
- ☐ Paper
- ☐ Paper clips
- ☐ Paper cutter (for trimming brochures, postcards, etc.)
- ☐ Pens, pencils, markers, and erasers
- ☐ Post-it notes
- ☐ Postage stamps
- ☐ Rubber bands
- ☐ Ruler
- ☐ Stapler and staples
- ☐ Tape
- ☐ Tape recorder (for practicing presentations)
- ☐ Time management planner, software, or handheld digital assistant

Furniture

- ☐ Bookcases for reference material
- ☐ Chair (one for you, and one for any employees, or clients who visit)
- ☐ Desk (one or more)
- ☐ Filing cabinet
- ☐ Lamps and lighting
- ☐ Storage shelves
- ☐ Work table (for handling mailings or putting together packets of material)

Telephones

The etiquette consultant's telephone is their business lifeline. In fact, you will probably have a business telephone and a cell phone, both of which are important business tools. If you chose to have a home office, you can install a second personal line and use it as your business line. However, if you choose to have a business line, then you will pay a little more, but your number will be listed in Yellow Pages and may bring you additional business.

An additional phone line is almost essential in today's business world, if only for a fax line. Also, an additional line is important if you spend time on the Internet and have dial-up service. You want your clients to be able to reach you.

You will most likely want to add a cellular phone to this mix as well. You can use your cell phone to check your messages and return business calls while you're out drumming up more business. Your cell phone is a lifesaver when you find yourself lost on the way to an important meeting. That quick call to the receptionist can save you from being late and blowing it with a potential client.

Most likely you will use voicemail when you first start the business. Make your voicemail message personal and engaging, and change your message regularly. Some people choose to put on a new message each day. Remember that the way in which your telephone is answered is extremely important. You're the etiquette expert and the first impression a potential client has of your business is when they call your number. Make certain that your telephone is always answered correctly. For a refresher, review section 2.1.5 on telephone etiquette.

Computer and Software

The first thing on the tech list is a computer, but considering the format of this book, you probably have one. Make sure you have the latest antivirus software, and consider business versions of programs you currently use, as well as the following:

- **Accounting software:** Quicken, QuickBooks, and Microsoft Money offer good bookkeeping software.
- **Desktop publishing software:** Microsoft Publisher, Adobe InDesign and QuarkXpress are excellent desktop publishing programs you can use to make brochures and other business materials.
- **Database management software:** ACT!, FileMaker Pro, and MS Outlook all offer programs for tracking contacts, clients, and projects.

If you are planning to use a printer to generate letters, brochures, and other business documents, consider investing in a laser printer. While the printer is more expensive, the toner cartridges are not much more expensive than inkjet cartridges, and last four to six times longer. The laser printer also prints faster and the quality of the print exceeds that of inkjet. There is a drawback, though — no color printing unless you buy a very expensive one. But for your purposes, while color printing does add pizzazz to your documents, laser quality documents look more professional.

4.4 Employees and Contractors

When you first start your business you will handle it all, from answering the phones and dusting to pitching your services and billing clients. However, after some time you may decide to bring on additional people to help you with the day-to-day business operations, or to help you with seminars and workshops.

Some jobs you may want to consider outsourcing include:

- Creating brochures, flyers, advertisements, and other promotional materials
- Putting together workshop materials based on your information and guidelines
- Assembling proposal packages for potential clients
- Writing material for workshops or seminars
- Website design and maintenance.

Another contracting arrangement some etiquette consultants rely on is hiring experts when clients request training they are not qualified to do. For example, if your forte is dining etiquette, and your client wants to learn dining etiquette and a bit about international protocol, you might hire or partner with a protocol expert on contract to fill in for you in this area. This kind of strategic alliance is common in consulting businesses.

Employees

An employee, by definition:

- Is paid by the hour
- Can be fired at any time
- Receives instructions and training from you
- Receives employee benefits
- Provides services that are a part of the day-to-day operations, such as administrative assistance

Hiring an employee involves a landslide of paperwork. United States employers need to have separate payroll records, withhold federal income and Social Security taxes, withhold state income and possibly state disability taxes, prepare quarterly and year-end payroll tax returns, pay the employee's portion of Social Security taxes and unemployment taxes, generally purchase workers' compensation insurance, and prepare year-end earnings statements for each employee.

When it's time to bring in some help, you need to decide what works best for you, hiring employees or bringing in contractors. For more on working with employees and independent contractors check out:

- *Small Business Administration's StartUp Kit*
  www.sba.gov/starting/regulations.html#othercon

- *Canada Business Service Centres*
  http://bsa.cbsc.org (click on "Hiring Employees or Contractors" once you get past the main page)

- *Nolo*
  (Click on the "Business & Human Resources" tab, and then on "Human Resources")
  www.nolo.com

Independent Contractor

An independent contractor:

- Is paid by the job
- Can earn a profit or can suffer a loss in a given year
- Furnishes their own tools and materials for the job
- Works for more than one company
- Pays their own business and traveling expenses
- Sets their own working hours
- Invests in equipment and materials

If you decide to use an independent contractor to handle your overflow of business, you aren't required to handle quite as much paperwork. In the United States, you aren't required to withhold taxes and only have to file Form 1099 with the IRS when you pay a contractor more than $600 in one year.

> **TIP:** You can't bring on an administrative assistant and call them an "independent contractor" to avoid paperwork and charges. The IRS' stand is that an employee is an employee if they meet the criteria, regardless of what the employer calls them.

Working with independent contractors is often more cost-efficient than hiring full-time or even part-time employees. You might pay them a flat fee or an hourly rate.

Another option is to refer a client to another consultant or company (a "strategic partner") in return for a referral fee. For example, if you refer a client to a foreign language tutor, that strategic partner pays you a fee as a thank you for referring business to them that they otherwise would not have.

There are no firm guidelines for the amount of a referral fee. It can be whatever you negotiate with a particular strategic partner, and might be a percentage of what they earn from the referral (e.g. five percent to 20 percent) or a flat fee.

In the F*abJob Guide to Become an Image Consultant*, Michelle T. Sterling, AICI, of Global Image Group recommends that you set up an interview to see if a relationship is mutually beneficial. She suggests that before you go in for an interview, ask yourself:

- What type of clientele or niche does this potential partner serve?
- Does it match my clientele?
- What is the reputation of the company?
- Is the management team efficient and reliable?
- Is this an establishment that I want to work with?

Ask any of the contractors you are screening if they have past clients who can offer a recommendation. If they can't, that may be a tip-off to avoid making an alliance with this contractor.

4.5 Client Contracts

A contract or agreement covers you and the client by spelling out exactly what services you will perform, in what manner you will perform them, and the agreed-upon fees. You should create a standard contract or agreement before you land that first job, not after.

4.5.1 Developing Your Standard Contract

Your contract doesn't have to be long, involved, or filled with big, long, legal-sounding words. In fact, some etiquette consultants choose to use a "letter of intent" in the place of a fill-in-the-blanks contract. This is a letter that is sent to the client after the planning meeting, which outlines the services they will provide, when they will provide them and the fees that the company (or individual) has agreed to pay. The letter is sent to the client for their signature.

If you are doing one-on-one consultation for a corporation, you can adapt the sample contract on the next few pages as appropriate. Make sure the contract is between your company and the client's company (and not the individual employee).

If a company is hiring you for a training program, your contract will need more detail about the program. Some organizations will have their legal department create a contract, and you can review it with your lawyer to ensure it covers what you want.

One of the most important elements of a training contract is a clause specifying when you will be paid. Another important element is a cancellation clause, or a statement that explains what will happen if a training program is cancelled. For example, some trainers have a clause which says if the client cancels the program, for any reason, less than a certain number of days before the event (e.g. 30, 60, or 90 days), the client forfeits the deposit.

No matter what form of contract you decide on, make sure you have one. A contract gives a more professional appearance to your business, and it covers you in case the person hiring you leaves the company or the company changes hands.

Sample Contract or Agreement

THIS AGREEMENT is made this [date] day of [month], 200__.

BETWEEN [insert name of your client] (the "Client"); and [insert your name or your company's name] (the "Etiquette Consultant"), collectively referred to as the "Parties."

1. Services
The Etiquette Consultant will provide the following services to the Client in accordance with the terms and conditions of this Agreement: [insert a description of the services]

2. Delivery of Services
Start date: [enter the start date]

Completion date: [enter the completion date]

3. Location
The Etiquette Consultant will provide these services at the following location(s): [enter the locations of the consultations, training, seminars/workshops]

4. Fees
As consideration for the services by the Etiquette Consultant, the fees for these services are [insert fees here] ("Fees").

The Client [will, will not] pay for the expenses consisting of [insert description of expenses here, if client agreed to pay].

5. Payment
The Client agrees to pay the Fees to the Etiquette Consultant on the following dates: [enter specific dates or specify the time payment is to be made such as, on completion; or specify installment payments such as, one half due at specific time and balance due upon completion].

The Etiquette Consultant will invoice the Client for the Services provided to the Client [at the completion, monthly, quarterly].

6. Warranty
The Etiquette Consultant represents and warrants that it will perform the Services with reasonable skill and care.

7. Limitation of Liability
Subject to the Client's obligation to pay the Fees to the Etiquette Consultant, either Party's liability arising directly out of its obligations under this Agreement and every applicable part of it shall be limited in aggregate to the Fees.

8. Term and Termination
This Agreement will be effective on the date signed and continue until the completion date stated in section 2, unless terminated sooner. If the Client terminates the Agreement [amount of time, or any time] before the scheduled completion date, the Client will reimburse the Etiquette Consultant for all outstanding fees and expenses [or an agreed upon amount or percentage of the contract].

9. Confidentiality
Neither Party will disclose any information of the other which comes into its possession under or in relation to the Agreement and which is of a confidential nature.

10. Miscellaneous
The failure of either Party to enforce its rights under this Agreement at any time for any period shall not be construed as a waiver of such rights.

This Agreement constitutes the entire understanding between the Parties and supersedes all prior representations, negotiations, or understandings.

This Agreement shall be governed by the laws of the jurisdiction in which the Client is located.

Agreed by the Parties hereto:

SIGNED by ____________________________________

on behalf of ____________________________________

[the Client]

SIGNED by ____________________________________

on behalf of ____________________________________

[the Etiquette Consultant]

Sample Training Contract

(On Your Letterhead)

Client
Jane Jones
Human Resources Department
XYZ Corporation
123 Main Street
Sunnyday, CA 90123

Purpose
To deliver a Training program for XYZ Corporation.

Details
The training sessions will be presented at the XYZ Center in Sunnyday. The training will consist of three half day (three hour) sessions scheduled to take place from 4:30 p.m. to 7:30 p.m. The session topics and dates are as follows:

Business Etiquette Basics	May 9, 2007
Dining Etiquette	May 16, 2007
International Protocol	May 23, 2007

The trainer will be Elaine Etiquette. In the event the chosen trainer is unavailable for a particular session, Elaine Etiquette Consulting Services will send a suitable and equally qualified trainer.

Client Responsibilities
- facility arrangements
- A/V equipment

Trainer Responsibilities
- printed materials for each participant
- delivery of training

Fees
Per session fee (based on 12 participants): $1,200.00 plus tax, payable within ten days after each session.

Actual billing may vary should the number of attendees exceed those quoted above. The minimum amount of program fees above, based on client's statement of numbers is binding, even when fewer participants actually attend.

If prior to the commencement of the program, dates are postponed or sessions cancelled, Elaine Etiquette Consulting Services shall be paid the appropriate postponement/cancellation charge as noted following.

(This does not apply to rescheduling of the order of topics or session start/end times, which may be changed on request.)

Days Prior to Scheduled Session	Postponement	Cancellation
30–90	10%	25%
11–29	25%	50%
10 or fewer	50%	75%

Signature and Date

Signed by: ______________________________ **Date:** ________

Jane Jones,
Vice President of Human Resources
XYZ Corporation

Signed by: ______________________________ **Date:** ________

Elaine Etiquette,
President
Elaine Etiquette Consulting Services Ltd.

4.5.2 Getting Paid

As a new business owner, you want to be sure that you'll get paid in a timely manner. The most important thing is to arrange for payment before you perform any service, so there are no misunderstandings in this department.

Deposits and Retainers

It's acceptable to ask for a deposit (pre-payment) or retainer (monthly fee) for a large project. Without a retainer you may not ever see your fee, and without a written cancellation policy you may not ever get paid for the work you completed.

Suppose you are asked to create a two-hour customized workshop on business, phone, and communication etiquette for a large corporation and present this workshop to over 200 employees over a two-week period. Your initial investment could be very substantial, considering the cost to create and print specific materials to hand out to over 200 employees. You want to make sure that you will at least recoup your expenses if the contract is terminated.

You can request a retainer when the work will take several months to complete or will cause you to incur large expenses. According to *Entrepreneur*, the average consulting retainer is $3,500 per month.

Many large organizations have a policy of paying 30 days after you send them an invoice, but may be willing to give you a deposit if you ask. Professional speakers sometimes ask to get paid in full on the day they speak. Others ask for half the speaking fee up front to hold the date, with a check for the balance at or before the speaking event.

Also consider including a cancellation policy as part of your contract or agreement, especially if you don't get a deposit or retainer. It covers you should a client decide that he doesn't want that specialized customer service training after you've invested hours researching his business.

Invoicing

Send out professional-looking invoices within one week of your work ending. Corporate clients are usually invoiced at the end of a training program, or they can be invoiced monthly if the training is ongoing. Your invoice should be on your letterhead and include the following:

- The client's name and contact information
- The date of the invoice
- A purchase order (PO) number if the client gave you one
- Services you provided
- Any expenses and taxes payable
- The total amount due
- Terms of payment (e.g. "Payable upon receipt" or "Payable within 30 days")

TIP: Some corporations use purchase order (PO) numbers to manage expenses. If a client uses purchase orders, they will either give you a paper copy or your contact person at the company will tell you the purchase order number.

Send your invoices promptly. You don't want to wait six months and send an invoice only to find out that the executive who you worked with has left the company. If you haven't received a check within 30 days, make a follow-up phone call.

Sample Invoice

(On Your Letterhead)

To: Jane Jones
Human Resources Department
City of Sunnyday
123 Main Street
Sunnyday, CA 90211

INVOICE

PO #: 1234

Date: April 14, 2007

Re: Etiquette Consulting Services

4/12/2007	Business Etiquette Workshop (2 hours @ $500 per hour)	$ 1,000.00
	Business Etiquette Workshop (Materials for 10 people @ $25 each)	250.00
4/14/2007	Business Etiquette Private Consultation (2 hours @ $100 per hour)	200.00
	Subtotal	$ 1,450.00
	10% tax *(include your own tax rate here)*	145.00
	Total – Please pay this amount	**$ 1,595.00**

Terms: Payable within 30 days.

Thank you for your business.

5. Getting Clients

With all the business matters taken care of, it's time to concentrate on finding people who will pay you for your etiquette knowledge and insight. There are many people who could use your skills, but they need to know who you are and what you can do for them. In this chapter you'll learn how to market your business and get clients.

5.1 Choose Your Target Market

Before you start trying to sell your services to prospective clients, you should decide which types of clients you want to work for. These are your "target" markets.

It can be tempting for a new consultant to say "I want to work for anyone who'll pay me!" However, it is costly and time-consuming to try to market your business to "everyone" and the truth is that some people will be more interested than others in the services you have to offer. In fact, people are more likely to hire you if they see you as an expert who specializes in what they need.

When you are just starting out, of course you might take whatever business comes your way. However, you can focus your marketing efforts (the time and money you invest to promote your business) on the target markets you most want to work with. Once you start getting more business, you may be able to give up work you find less rewarding, and spend your time on the etiquette consulting you find most rewarding.

One of the best ways to help you decide where to focus your marketing efforts is to choose a "niche" or specialty. You can review the different etiquette specialties described earlier in this guide, and think about what of these areas most appeals to you, or is complemented by your skills and experience. For example, past experience working with children, or having children of your own, might lend itself well to a career specialty in children's etiquette. As you research and learn more about etiquette consulting, take note of areas that appeal to you.

Once you know your niche, you can then identify which businesses or individuals would be most interested in that service. Ask yourself "Who would be willing to pay to learn this?" For example:

- If you decide to specialize in international protocol, you could focus on marketing your services to companies that are doing business with overseas clients.

- If your specialty is social etiquette your target market might be young executives who want to advance in their careers.

- You might decide to specialize in telephone etiquette and focus on marketing your services to businesses with call centers.

As you get more experience you may decide to go after new target markets, or your business may naturally evolve to focus on particular types of clients. However, starting with some specific target markets in mind can help you focus your marketing efforts most efficiently—saving you both time and money.

In this chapter you will learn about a variety of marketing techniques you can use to reach your target market. However, before you begin using those marketing techniques, there are a variety of promotional tools you should consider developing so you have them available when meeting with prospective clients.

5.2 Promotional Tools

Promotional tools are materials that you can use to tell people about your exciting new business.

5.2.1 Business Cards

The first thing on your list of promotional tools is your business cards. This is the one item that you can't do without.

Your business card should be a reflection of you and your business. In other words, you should avoid gimmicks and bright colors, but stick with cards that appear classy and professional. If possible, invest in a sturdy card that has a good weight and feel to it. People do notice this. You also want to make sure that your business card gives enough information to let people know what you do. It can include:

- Your name and title
- Your company name
- Contact information (phone number, email address, fax number, web address)
- Your specializations
- Professional credentials (see the next page for ideas)

You can see a variety of ways to present information on your business card at VistaPrint, which offers 250 business cards for only $19.95. Go to the *VistaPrint Business Cards* site at **www.vistaprint.com** and follow the links provided.

Professional Credentials

Make sure you mention your credentials in all of your promotional materials. For example, if you have taken any of the etiquette certification programs listed in section 2.3.1, you can indicate that you are a Certified Professional Etiquette Consultant or whatever designation you have earned from the company that provided your certification training.

If you have any other professional or educational credentials, such as a relevant graduate degree, you could include it after your name (e.g. Mary Manners, MBA).

Another impressive credential is membership in a professional association. Following are three organizations to consider, which you can join on an annual basis. They all offer a variety of member benefits including publications and events, which are described on their websites.

International Association of Protocol Consultants

Membership in IAPC is open to all consultants and other professionals involved with protocol and etiquette. You can join now as an IAPC Associate or Professional Member for $695 for the first year and $595 per year thereafter, if you meet the education and experience requirements described at their website.

Website: **www.protocolconsultants.org** (click "Join IAPC")

Phone: (703) 759-4272

Email: information@protocolconsultants.org

International Society of Protocol and Etiquette Professionals

ISPEP is an organization for professional trainers and consultants dealing with international protocol, corporate etiquette, and business communications. You can join as an Active member for $325 once you have been in the industry for more than three years. Until then, you can join as an Apprentice member for $195.

Your membership fee includes distribution of a press release to 500 publications relevant to your area of expertise, geographic location or target audience.

Website: **www.ispep.org**
Phone: (301) 946-5265
Email: info@ispep.org

Association of Image Consultants International (AICI)

Image consultants offer training, both one-on-one and in seminar settings, on the overall image a person presents. While some image consultants specialize in helping people improve their appearance, others provide etiquette consulting services and advise clients on communication skills. You can join as an Associate Member for $275.

Website: **www.aici.org/find/finding.htm**
Phone: (630) 655-2424
Email: info@aici.org

5.2.2 Website

Having a website is a must in today's competitive market. A website gives your potential clients a way to "look" at your business before they ever meet you or talk with you. This is a way for potential clients to check you out from their office, 24 hours a day.

If your budget is limited, you may be able to put up free web pages through your Internet service provider (the company that gives you access to the Internet). Contact them for details about how to put up your own website. It will probably have an address like: **www.yourinternetcompany.com/yourpages/index.html**

If you can afford it, it's preferable to get your own domain name, such as www.yourname.com because it makes you appear to be more serious about your consulting career. There are a number of sites where you can search for and register a domain name. One such site is GoDaddy. You can find them at **www.godaddy.com**.

Once you register your domain, you will need to find a place to "host" it. Your Internet service provider may offer that service. You can find a wide variety of other companies that provide hosting services by doing an online search for "website hosting."

You can design your own web pages using a program like Microsoft FrontPage, or hire someone to design your site for you. Check your favorite search engine or your local Yellow Pages under "Internet." Remember to ask for references and get a price quote in writing. Remember that regular updates are a must, so see if they are willing to provide ongoing service as well.

If you design your own website, keep the following key tips in mind:

- Include catchy content. You want your text to matter. Give the people who visit your site something to read. Many etiquette consultants offer an etiquette quiz on their sites, which is fun and entertaining.

- Use a simple, balanced design. You want your website to be a balance of graphics and text. Too much text looks boring and dull. But too many graphics makes for slow loading time. Also, the overall look of your site should be a reflection of you and your services. For many etiquette consultants, that means a look that is classy, elegant, and professional.

- Make the site easy to use. You want anyone visiting your site to be able to move around easily. Make it simple to find other areas on your site with just a click of a mouse button.

The following items at your website can help establish your credibility:

- Your photograph: a headshot and some photos of you "in action" presenting a workshop to an audience are ideal.

- A summary of your training programs and the benefits they offer to potential clients.

- Testimonials from satisfied clients (covered in section 5.4.3).

- Useful general information about etiquette, such as articles, stories, or quotations to add to your credibility and give potential employers a sense of your style.

- Audio or video "samples" of your training sessions or seminars.

- A way to contact you, including at least your company name, telephone number and email address. (This should be on every page.)

- To build up a contact list, you could offer a free email newsletter, and include a place at your website where visitors can subscribe.

5.2.3 Brochures

A brochure gives people a snapshot of what your business is all about. Some etiquette consultants choose to develop very detailed brochures while others prefer a clean look with less detail. At the very least your brochure should include:

- Your business name and contact information
- Your web address
- Your photo
- A description of your professional qualifications
- A sampling of your workshops or services
- A description of the takeaway value (what benefit people will get)

You may also want to include quotes or testimonials from past workshop participants (see section 5.4.3 for sample testimonials).

The cost for having brochures printed can range from a few thousand dollars (if you opt for the color and glossy paper) to a few hundred (for one color on cardstock). Spend time on the copy and layout of your brochure, working with a designer if necessary.

Many printers will have an in-house design department who can do the artwork for you, but make sure you have a hand in developing the text. You are the best qualified person to describe what you can do for a client. Also check your phone number, email address, and other contact information carefully to make sure there are no typos, or you will be paying the printer to fix 1000 brochures, or staying up until 3:00 a.m. doing it yourself.

You may be tempted to print your own brochures on your home computer and you can with brochure papers available at stationery stores such as Staples or Office Depot. But make sure that you create a professional-looking brochure. You want something that you are proud to have your name associated with.

5.2.4 Portfolio

A portfolio is a collection of samples of your work, plus any other documents that can show people why they should hire you. A portfolio is not essential for an etiquette consultant to have, but it can help you stand out from other applicants, and prove that you have the skills to do the job. Your portfolio might include:

- Samples of work you have done such as written materials from an etiquette workshop you presented

- Samples created for your portfolio

- Other materials that provide evidence of your expertise

There are no rules about what to include in your portfolio. The main thing to remember is to choose items that you think are likely to impress someone who could hire you. If you have created several etiquette programs, you could include an outline of each program. Alternatively, you could include an overview of each workshop, with the title, brief description, and presentation time length. You might also include some handout materials.

> **TIP:** If you are a new consultant without any experience, you can still create a small portfolio of one or more workshops you plan to offer, with appropriate handouts. A sample workshop outline is included in section 5.4.3 of this book.

In addition to training materials, your portfolio can include:

- A cover page with your name and contact information

- A resume or profile (see section 5.4.3 for a sample profile)

- A copy of any etiquette certificates

- Any articles written by or about you from newspapers or magazines

- Testimonials from clients

Be selective about what you include. A portfolio of 12 to 16 pages in length is enough for a client to review during a meeting. (Don't leave a portfolio with a client unless you have copies of everything.)

Copy materials onto high quality white or cream colored paper, then place them in an attractive three-ring binder or two pocket folder. (All these materials are available from stationery stores such as Staples or Office Depot.)

5.3 Marketing Techniques

In this section we'll look at a variety of marketing techniques, ranging from networking and speaking engagements to advertising and free publicity. Some of these techniques will help you connect with individuals for consultation, or may help you break into larger corporations for seminars. In any event, they are designed to spread the word that you are an etiquette expert, and that you are willing to share this expertise with clients.

5.3.1 Networking

Word of mouth can be the best and cheapest marketing tool you have, but you have to let people know who you are and what you do to get them talking about you. Networking gives you that chance, and networking opportunities are almost limitless.

Before you race out the door with business cards in hand, let's take a look at how networking truly works. Certainly you will need those business cards, but you also need a bit more preparation.

It's a good idea to create a "tag line" to introduce yourself that easily identifies what you do, but also is intriguing enough to get people to ask you questions about what you do. You could use something like:

> "I'm Betty Etiquette, and I help make people more confident."
>
> "I'm Bob Etiquette, and I teach people which fork to use."
>
> "I'm Elaine Etiquette, and I teach people how to hand out business cards."

The first tagline is more formal and intriguing, while the last two are more fun and interesting. Any of these three will usually cause people to ask questions about your business, and it opens the door to discussion.

Once you've had the chance to talk a bit about your business, make certain to ask about the other person's business and listen. As you know from your etiquette training, it's important not to let your eyes begin to scan the room looking for your next potential client. Remember, the person in front of you is the most important person in the room, at least, while they are in front of you. Meeting people is the first step to networking.

However, you often have to dig a bit deeper (and offer to work a little harder) to reap the greatest networking benefits.

Volunteering for Committees

Most networking relationships come through committee work. This is where you roll up your sleeves and spend time in the trenches with other people. These people see your work ethic and you get to know each other very well, and this is when networking begins to pay off. Here is a short list of groups you can network within:

- Chamber of Commerce
- Business organizations, such as small business organizations
- Sales clubs
- Networking clubs
- Service clubs, such as Lions Club or Rotary Club
- Charity events (like fundraisers for health issues or fundraisers for children and children's services)
- Arts councils and clubs

Be sure to target the groups that will benefit your business the most. If you are planning on teaching children's or teen's etiquette, then it's a good idea to build a relationship with the area school districts, educators, and staff.

Endorsements and Referrals

Referrals are the lifeblood of most businesses and the etiquette consulting business isn't any different. People like to tell their friends and associates about a new discovery, so why not take advantage of it? This is the conversation that will get you the business:

> "Hey, I just went to this really useful workshop on cell phone etiquette. The trainer was fun, and I had no idea how many people I was probably annoying with my bad cell phone habits. You should get her to do something for your organization — here's her card, she gave us a bunch to pass along."

Don't be shy about asking for referrals. If a happy client tells you how they enjoyed your seminar or what a great impact you had on their staff, ask for that referral. Try this line: "Do you know some others who would be interested in a workshop [or the service you provided]?"

Once you get that "yes," ask if you may call these people and use their name. There is nothing wrong with this tactic and it makes for good business. If people are pleased with your services, they will want others to know about it. Also, ask if you may repeat their comments. Again, people are often pleased to offer this assistance.

Once you have the referral name in hand and the endorsement from a happy customer, it's time to start making those phone calls and lining up some more new happy clients. Here is a sample referral or endorsement call:

> "Hello, Mr. Jones. My name is Eileen Etiquette and I own an etiquette consulting business, Etiquette for Everyone. Sue Smith at Sid's Software suggested that I give you a call about the etiquette workshop I just completed for her inside sales staff. Sue said she noticed an immediate change in her staff and that customers have even called in to compliment her staff on their excellent phone skills. Sue mentioned your name and thought you might be interested in a similar workshop for your staff."

Don't worry if your prospective client puts you off at first. They may want to call your client and verify the situation for themselves. In section 5.4.2 you will learn what to do once you get through to the prospective client.

5.3.2 Speaking Engagements

Speaking engagements are opportunities for you to display your skills, put your name out into the community, and be seen as an expert.

Free Speeches and Workshops

There is a huge market for speakers on various aspects of etiquette. Service clubs, networking organizations, schools and social clubs frequently look for presentations for their members and students. It may be a 15-minute luncheon address on the subject of business entertaining, or may involve an interactive workshop for a school band traveling out of the country on a tour. To ensure your time giving free speeches is well spent, consider who your target audience is.

Speeches

There are many associations that meet on a regular basis and that are always on the lookout for speakers. Presenting your programs at local service, business, and special interest clubs will put your name and skills in front of the public. And you never know who will be in which club, so treat all opportunities to speak as a chance to reach the CEO of the biggest company in town.

You can look in your local paper for information on club meetings (check in the section that has the local news happenings). There is almost always a phone number to contact for more information. Also, many of these groups are local chapters of national organizations and you can find information on these local chapters at the national website. Look for officers' names and contact information. Here are some possibilities for speaking engagements:

- **Service Clubs:** These are service organizations, such as Lions Clubs (**www.lionsclubs.org**), Rotary International (**www.rotary.org**), Kiwanis (**www.kiwanis.org**), and Civitan (**www.civitan.org**), which have local community chapters. Check with your area Chamber of Commerce for the contact information of the local service clubs. These clubs meet monthly and are always looking for interesting speakers. You can check with your local Chamber of Commerce for information on the local service clubs in your area, and don't forget to ask family and friends for referrals.

- **Chamber of Commerce:** Call your local chamber, as well as those of the other towns or cities that surround you. Ask to speak to the person in charge of events and speakers. Many chambers have monthly gatherings and are often looking for speakers.

- **The PTA:** Parent Teacher Associations are often on the lookout for fun and informative speakers. Call the local schools and ask the receptionist for contact information of the current PTA president. Schools are often strapped for money and always on the lookout for low-cost training. You may want to offer to do a short program at a staff meeting, school assembly or a PTA meeting in return for the chance to market your business.

Prepare a brief but informative pitch on you and your services. For example:

> "Hi, Mr. Jones. I understand that you handle speakers for the Lions Club. My name is Mary Smedwith and I'm a professional etiquette consultant. I would love the chance to come and speak to your club. I have several short presentations on a variety of topics from knowing which fork to use to holiday etiquette. May I put you on my calendar?

If you are met with an enthusiastic "Yes, we would love to have you," then you have won half the battle. The next step is to present a program that helps generate business for your consulting services. When you are presenting to these types of groups you will need something short, fun, and informative. You want to whet their appetite for more etiquette training. Remember to send a note thanking them for allowing you to speak and offering your services in the future.

You can develop talks on any subject you specialize in. You could create a presentation on a topic such as "Etiquette Through the Ages" to show the changes in etiquette through the years. However, most audiences prefer information they can use to improve their lives. "Email Etiquette" programs may be more popular because this is an area that is confusing for many people. Likewise, you can create seasonal talks, such as a "Christmas Party Etiquette Savvy" program to have on hand around the holidays.

Service organizations tend to enjoy entertaining presentations that appeal to the diverse membership. Deportment and body language, especially in a cultural context, is always popular, as are presentations on formal dress and dining, etiquette for specific venues such as weddings, funerals and even divorce; and conduct for sport (sailing, golf, polo) are well received.

And don't forget the subjects you can present with a dash of humor, such as etiquette for motorists. (You can always find amusing stories, such as the fellow who, running late for an interview and desperate for a parking space, pulled into a reserved stall, only to discover that he'd snitched the spot allotted to his prospective employer!) Teaching manners to children and pets are great topics, and technology has opened up a whole new world of behavioral dilemmas (can you email a sympathy card? Fax a thank-you note? Extend a wedding invitation by telephone? Post your Christmas greetings on a website?)

Mini Workshops

In addition to speeches, consider giving mini-workshops. A one-hour workshop could bring you great return in business from your investment of time. Here are a few ideas:

- **Communicating with Class:** "Everyone uses email, cell phones, and voicemail and the rules of etiquette aren't often clear among these newer forms of communication."

- **Hosting 101:** "Handling a dinner party or a business event takes more than just the ability to call on a good caterer. This seminar can teach the finer points of party and event hosting."

- **Networking Etiquette**: "Handing out a business card and shaking hands can be filled with pitfalls if you're unsure of just what to do. The art of shaking hands, how to introduce people, and how to make small talk are just a sampling of the topics you will cover."

- **Dining Etiquette:** "Learn what each piece of silverware is used for and the drinks that will be poured into each glass. Also, you can review the art of dinner party conversation."

- **Etiquette for Teens:** "Covers a wide variety of topics including cellular phone etiquette, dining etiquette, introductions, and conversational skills for teens. You'll address issues that face teens such as, how to introduce your parents to your date."

- **Graduation and Beyond:** "Seniors in high school and college are excited about what's next, and also a bit nervous about what's to come. These workshops cover interviewing skills, telephone skills, office etiquette, appropriate business attire, and communication etiquette."

Many of the groups that you might do speeches for may also be interested in a workshop. However, you should also consider other opportunities to present mini-workshops to your target market. For example, if you are targeting young executives who might be interested in your social etiquette consulting services, identify the club or organization that is the "in" group for young executives and offer a free mini-workshop.

Contact the club and ask to speak to the person in charge of special events and programs. This may be the club manager or it may be the events coordinator. By asking for the person who handles programs, you quickly find out just who you need to talk with. Once you have this person on the phone, introduce yourself and explain that you would like a chance to present a workshop to the club members free of charge. An introduction of yourself when you first make contact might go something like this:

> "Hi, I'm Susan Watkins. I'm a professional etiquette consultant and I would love the chance to do a short presentation for your group. I have several fun and informative mini-workshops that I think your group would enjoy. Can I send you some information?"

Likewise, if a certain company in town is known for hiring the best and the brightest, then you may want to get your foot in the door by contacting the company's human resources department to offer a free workshop in return for the right to leave your promotional materials.

Teach a Class or Course

Teaching etiquette to adults can be done in a classroom setting at local community colleges, or another type of continuing education facility. It gives you the chance to build your skills and your confidence in a more casual setting. Also, the community school or college will likely add your course to the catalog, and this helps to get your name out into the community. Use adult etiquette courses to teach the basics, and give people an interest in learning more.

Check with your local community college or continuing education program about getting on the upcoming schedule. The first step is to review the current catalog of continuing education courses offered by local colleges, universities and other organizations that provide adult education classes in your community. Call and ask for a print catalog if they do not have course information at their website.

Once you have reviewed their current list of courses, come up with some ideas for new courses. (They already have instructors for any courses that are in their catalog.)

Once you have an idea for a new course in mind, call the college or organization and ask to speak with whoever hires continuing education instructors. Once you connect with the right person, let them know your profession and offer to teach courses for the program. You will have to develop your own curriculum within the institution's guidelines. You might also be asked to set your own hours and your fees per person.

Another idea is to partner with a cooking school or class to provide food for a dining etiquette class. You can trade services, like possibly teaching an interview skills class to the culinary students in return for their services.

If you have enough material to teach a class or course, why not increase your income while attracting clients by offering etiquette seminars or workshops to the public. Because there are quite a few logistics involved in presenting your own seminars or workshops, this topic is covered in depth in the next section.

5.3.3 Present Your Own Seminars or Workshops

Seminars can be a fabulous way to earn extra money for your business, and promote your services to future clients.

Planning your first seminar is similar to planning a big party. Of course, one main difference is that you are the entertainment, and people are paying to hear you speak. When you present your own seminar you pay the bills and handle the administrative details, but you can also reap large rewards.

Establish a Planning Timeline

How you set up your timeline will depend on the amount of time you have to plan your seminar. Ideally you need several weeks — a month or more is better if you are handling all the details such as finding space, advertising, registering, etc. Here is a breakdown of a standard timeline, which you'll want to adjust to fit your specific situation:

- Set a date and time
- Find a location
- Select a topic and create training materials
- Set fees and deadline for registration
- Identify publicity opportunities
- Present your seminar

Choose a Date and Time

The *FabJob Guide to Become a Motivational Speaker* by Tag Goulet includes a detailed section on putting on seminars, and offers the following great advice on choosing a date and time:

Don't worry too much about choosing the wrong date. Low turn-outs are often blamed on the wrong date, but I believe few seminars fail for this reason alone. You can hold a seminar at almost any time of year and, regardless of what else is going on at the same time, have an excellent turn-out if you are offering something people are genuinely interested in.

Likewise, if people are not interested in the topic, it does not matter how convenient your date and time are.

Best Months for Seminars

Although you can hold seminars at almost any time of the year, some dates are better than others. It seems that people of all ages are ready to "go back to school" in September and January. For many seminar presenters, September is the best month for registrations, while January is next best. While the number of registrations will depend on many factors besides the date, we have found that if we get 50 registrations for a seminar in April or November, we may get 150 in September and 100 in late January.

You should avoid late December because people are busy with the holiday season. To maximize registrations also stay away from any statutory holidays or long weekends, and avoid competing with popular local events.

Best Days of the Week

The day of the week is also an important factor in getting registrations. If organizations will be paying to send their employees to the seminar, the seminar can be held any weekday during business hours (Tuesday, Wednesday, and Thursday are best).

If participants are paying their own way, you'll have the best turnout if you schedule the seminar for a Saturday or an evening.

Best Times of Day

For participants who are attending on their own time, an evening seminar is usually easier to fit into their schedule than a Saturday seminar. The difference in registrations can be dramatic. It is not unusual to get twice as many registrants for an evening seminar as for a full-day seminar. An evening seminar can be scheduled to start at 6:00, 6:30 or 7:00 p.m., and should ideally end no later than 10:00 p.m. with one or two coffee breaks.

Daytime seminars should ideally start no earlier than 8:00 a.m. on a weekday or 9:00 a.m. on a Saturday, with registration starting a half hour or an hour before that (depending on the number of participants). Consider taking your lunch break at 11:45 a.m. so participants can beat the rush at local restaurants, and allow for at least one coffee break in both the morning and afternoon.

If you want your audience to stay with you, mentally as well as physically, make sure you finish no later than 5:00 p.m. It's even better if you can finish by 4:00 p.m. No matter how interested participants are, it can be difficult to remain attentive through a program of much more than six hours (seven hours, including lunch).

Seminar Location

You can hold public seminars in a variety of places, but you may want something inexpensive, easily accessible by anyone who wants to attend, and in a location that will bring in the most people. Possibilities include:

- Banks
- Bookstores
- Churches and Synagogues
- Clubhouses at apartment complexes
- Coffee shops
- Libraries
- Office meeting rooms or cafeterias
- Restaurants
- Schools

TIP: If you want to book a room at a restaurant try to schedule from 2:00 p.m. to 4:00 p.m., which are quieter times for the restaurant, and consider bartering your training services for free room rental.

The location of your seminar will be an indicator of what people can expect. If you're hoping to catch the eye of the buttoned-up financial industry, you wouldn't hold a seminar for this group at a local YMCA. However, if you want to do business with up and coming professionals, you may want to consider holding an event at the local popular coffee shop or bookstore.

Using a good hotel or popular convention center can give your seminar credibility among potential registrants. These facilities also have employees who can advise you on room layouts, handle room setup, and book audio-visual equipment.

To Discuss with Catering Coordinator

- ☐ Room layout
- ☐ Start and end times (and if you need earlier access to the room)
- ☐ Registration table (inside or outside room, number of chairs)
- ☐ Additional tables inside the room for literature, displays, etc.
- ☐ Coat rack or coat check
- ☐ Audio-visual equipment (depending on your own needs)
    - ☐ microphone (clip-on is best for moving around)
    - ☐ overhead projector
    - ☐ flipchart or white board and markers
    - ☐ TV/VCR/DVD Player
    - ☐ sound system
    - ☐ plug-in for lap-top computer
- ☐ Stage or risers (so all participants can see you)
- ☐ Notepads and pens or pencils for participants
- ☐ Coffee service
- ☐ Meals or snacks
- ☐ Delivery arrangements (if you need to ship supplies to the hotel)
- ☐ Availability of parking for you and participants
- ☐ Access to public transportation
- ☐ Posting on hotel bulletin board (organization or seminar title)
- ☐ Your phone number for people to call if they have inquiries

If you are booking a meeting room at a hotel or convention center, you will need to speak with someone in the sales or catering office. (If you're booking a room at a facility such as a library, ask the receptionist to put you through to the person responsible for renting meeting rooms.) The catering coordinator will ask you the date of your seminar, how many people you expect, and what room layout you want.

A room laid out in "theater style" (chairs only), will allow you to fit at least twice as many people into a room as "classroom style" (tables and chairs), but if your participants will do a lot of writing or if you expect a small group, arrange for tables. If you don't know how many people to expect, or if there's a possibility the seminar may be cancelled, try to book the facility on a tentative basis until you are sure it will go ahead.

> **TIP:** You may be able to reduce the rental cost for your meeting room simply by asking. If the price is high, tell them you are on a budget and ask if they can do any better on the price. If the facility is not booked, they may be willing to make a deal. We have had the price reduced by up to 50% at many facilities.

Unless you are presenting a dining tutorial, a meal is not necessary. However, your participants will appreciate refreshments such as coffee, tea, bottled water, and juice. It's a nice touch to serve muffins and fruit in the morning, and cookies for an afternoon snack—but it's not required.

Select a Topic and Create Training Materials

The types of seminars that you present will depend on personal preferences and the most popular topics in your area, or may be specific to the location you have chosen. Once you have chosen a topic, follow the steps outlined in section 3.3.4 to write and develop your material.

Set Your Registration Deadline and Fee

When choosing a registration deadline, you'll need enough time to ensure that you have materials for everyone attending. Ten days before the event is a good rule of thumb. You should also have a cancellation policy in place that covers a percentage of the fee, should a registrant decide at the last minute not to attend.

Some seminars will leave registration open until the last minute, which can pay off, especially if registration is still low by your cut-off date. If you run an ad for a free or inexpensive public seminar ($49 or less) several days before the event, you may get as many as 50 percent of your registrations from "walk-ins": people who show up at the door. (But don't count on them, either, as it depends on what is going on the same day.)

When someone approaches the registration desk, ask if they have pre-registered. If they have not, ask their name and how they would like to pay for the seminar.

If you plan to interact with your group, keep the number small and manageable. Participation from a group of ten is one thing, but participation from a group of fifty is much more difficult to manage.

If your goal is to make money, some things to consider when setting your fee are who your audience is, whether you are offering valuable information that isn't available from other sources, and how confident you are in your ability to convince people of the seminar's value. If other etiquette consultants offer similar programs, you can check out their fees by reviewing their website.

If you are not concerned about making a profit from the seminar, you may want to consider charging only a nominal registration fee or even offering it free to all or some of the participants. Assuming the topic is an interesting one, this tactic may help to draw a crowd. Having a large audience can make a good impression on decision-makers who attend as guests.

Consider using free public seminars as an opportunity to whet the appetite of those wanting more information (and more training) on etiquette. You might want to do brief lectures (5–10 minutes) on specific etiquette areas such as dining etiquette, communication etiquette, cellular etiquette, business etiquette, and international etiquette.

> **TIP:** If you are offering any free seminars, you will still need to require registration. This serves two purposes: first, you get the name and contact information of everyone attending to add to your contact list, and second, you can limit the attendance to a manageable number of people.

Publicize Your Event

Getting the word out to the right people can make or break your event. You may decide to do mailings to local businesses or send out flyers or brochures. Do this a few weeks before the deadline to register for the event, and follow up with key contacts by phone.

If your local newspaper offers free listings for upcoming events, make sure to get yours in on time. Send it in about a month before it should run, unless your paper has a different deadline schedule. Also, contact radio stations and television stations with your information several weeks before the event.

The best way to market an upcoming seminar (with the greatest number of registrations for the lowest cost) is to get a feature story about it published in a local newspaper. Contact lifestyle editors or columnists and invite them to hear you speak at an event before the seminar.

5.3.4 Advertising

Paying for advertising ensures that you send the message you want to people in the media of your choice. While some forms of advertising (such as television) are simply not cost-effective for etiquette consultants, the following work for some:

Yellow Pages

Etiquette consultants are found in the Yellow Pages under "business consultants," "consultants," and sometimes even under "etiquette consultants." As a rule, Yellow Pages ads don't bring a lot of business to etiquette consultants, but that doesn't mean that it won't work for you. If someone does respond to your ad, they may be "shopping around," so you must be prepared to invest time as well as advertising dollars if you use this method of advertising.

If you decide to try an ad in the Yellow Pages, you may want to consider something business-card size. Also, look around for a Yellow Pages alternative, as many areas have competing telephone directories and these can offer similar ad space for less money. (Make sure you check into the circulation of the alternative directory, though!)

You can either design the ad yourself, have the Yellow Pages design it for you, or hire a designer. Take a look at the ads in the events category of your current Yellow Pages for ideas. If you are interested in advertising, contact your local Yellow Pages to speak with a sales rep. Check the print version of your phone book for contact information.

Magazines

Magazine advertising can be expensive, and may not generate the results you want unless you do it repeatedly. (It has been estimated that many people need to see an advertisement three to seven times before they buy.)

If you choose to buy advertising, it will probably be most cost-effective to place ads in small local magazines or newspapers aimed at your target market. The publications you advertise in will usually design your ad for an additional cost, and give you a copy of the ad to run in other publications. Here are some tips for effective advertising:

- Make your ad about your customers. Explain how they can benefit from your services rather than just listing the services you provide.

- Ask for the sale, and make contacting you easy. Provide your contact information in an easy-to-read or easy-to-find format.

- Create professional quality work. Don't try to create a cheap ad campaign because it shows and reflects poorly on you.

- Make long-term plans for your advertising program. Chances are running an ad once won't give you as much business as you would hope. Develop a long-term advertising strategy for better results.

5.3.5 Free Publicity

If paying for a big ad campaign just isn't in your budget, don't worry. Many etiquette consultants never pay for advertising. This doesn't mean they don't have a media presence; it just means they don't pay to have it. Some of the best advertising you will ever get will be free. Here are some ideas for free media publicity which will position you as an etiquette expert.

Guest on a TV Program

Local TV producers are always on the lookout for good, entertaining, and informative guests, and you can create fun and entertaining segments for a local TV program. To identify the shows that you would like to target, look for morning shows, mid-day news shows or other shows that feature a variety of people on a variety of topics. Contact the station, ask for the name of the producer of the show and call them. Pitch your idea in less than 30 seconds.

Here's a quick script:

> "Hi Mr. Wallace. I was just watching *Good Morning Town* and saw the speech expert you had on. He was great. I'm a professional etiquette consultant and I would love to come on the show and do a short segment on different etiquette skills. We could cover dining etiquette, cell phone etiquette, business etiquette, and even email etiquette. Can we set up a meeting?"

Prepare for your meeting. Have three or four segments that are three to five minutes long ready to show the producer. Immediately after your meeting, send a thank-you card or letter, and if you don't have a firm answer in a week to ten days, call and follow up.

Write an Article or Column

One of the best ways to establish yourself as an expert is to write articles or a column for a newspaper, magazine, or newsletter. While it can be tough to break into large daily newspapers, there may be an opportunity to write for smaller publications.

You could write a general etiquette column for the lifestyle section of the local newspaper, a dining etiquette column for a local food magazine, a business etiquette column for the Chamber of Commerce Newsletter, or an "Ask the Etiquette Consultant" column where you would answer questions from readers. The length and frequency of your column will depend on the publication. You might produce a weekly 500-word column for a local newspaper, or a monthly 1,000-word column for a newsletter or magazine.

Sample Etiquette Column

Pet Peeves

by Lori Benjamin

Doesn't it seem that some perfectly polite people allow their pets to be rude for them?

I am fond of animals: Witness three retired greyhounds, two rescued cats, and assorted grand-ferrets, grand-rats and a hedgehog niece.

But I don't appreciate being jumped at, slobbered on, sniffed or scratched on the strength of a casual introduction.

I've heard parents threaten their children with disowning for being rude to guests, yet the same people smile indulgently as Fido filches the canapés and Fluffy shreds a brand new pair of stockings.

I will politely admire hamsters, gerbils, and other assorted rodents while they are decently corralled in their pens. Admiration is not the reaction they will get should they attempt to crawl up my leg.

Birds belong in cages while company is about. Not everyone enjoys Boris the budgie nesting in their hair, much less finding oneself the recipient of his little birdie souvenirs.

And as for exotic pets, I will take your word that your tarantula doesn't bite and Precious the Python isn't slimy. Really. Please do not demonstrate.

I've watched a young child positively gibbering with fear as a playful pet pig (yes, the oinking variety) wriggled and snuffed about, trying to entice the child to play. The pig's owners thought it was cute. I thought it was heartbreaking. I wonder whether they would be as tolerant if the child were terrorizing the pig?

It shouldn't have to be said that pet owners ought to clean up after their animals, but it clearly does. What could be more discourteous than letting your pet use your neighbour's lawn for a lavatory? And it's not only disgusting, it's illegal.

Owners who allow their pets to misbehave are not being fair. For it's the pet who bears the blame, though it's really not his fault.

Well behaved pets are a joy to be around. Those that can't be trained must be controlled. In the end, the secret to a well-behaved pet is a responsible, well- mannered owner.

Make sure your article or column provides valuable information to the publication's readers. As with press releases, articles that sound like an ad for your services are not likely to get published.

Contact the editor of the section you want to write for. Usually the editors and their phone numbers are noted in the publication, but if not, call the paper or journal and ask for the name and number of the editor of the section. Once you get the editor on the phone, offer to send a sample column (or several) and a list of column ideas.

If they want to publish it, they may offer to pay you. However, even if they don't pay, you should consider letting them publish it in return for including a brief bio and your contact information at the end of the article or column.

On the previous page is a sample "Mind Your Manners" column written by Lori Benjamin of World Class Etiquette. It is among hundreds of columns that she wrote over a number of years for the *Calgary Sun*, and several other Canadian newspapers. If you plan to write your own columns, this sample can show you what editors look for in an etiquette column. You'll notice the short paragraphs and simple language that many readers prefer.

Guest on a Radio Show

Offer to do on-air segments for radio. Create something entertaining that will work without visual aids. You can write a useful fact sheet to send to radio stations about etiquette, with your name and number prominently displayed. Make the facts interesting or unusual.

There are literally thousands of radio programs on every day, and probably quite a few programs right in your area that are looking to add something lively to their lineup. There are a variety of programs from the serious talk shows to the lighter morning shows, so if you are going to contact these shows keep your approach consistent with the style of show.

Contact the show's producers by calling the station and asking for the name or number of the producer to a specific show. Now you have the name. Use the same steps set out to contact a TV producer, and don't forget to follow up.

5.4 Targeting Corporate Clients

If you are trying to break into the corporate market, the best way to get hired is to become known as the local etiquette expert. The more you do the activities such as those described in section 5.3 (speaking engagements, writing a column, etc.), the more likely you are to be contacted by organizations that need etiquette training.

Some etiquette consultants also get work with corporate clients through direct contact — in other words, by picking up the phone and setting up meetings. However, even if an organization wants etiquette training, it may take months to break into that organization, so it is wise to approach as many prospective clients as possible if you decide to do this.

Once you are well on your way in your career, you can hire someone else for this task. But when you are just starting out, you'll want to make contact yourself. In this section you will learn how to get from a cold call to a winning proposal in the corporate market.

5.4.1 Creating Your Call List

Once you have decided to approach the corporate market, you should create a "wish list" of clients. These are the clients that you want to do business with. To create your wish list, start by identifying which types of organizations you want to target. Listed below are key types of corporate clients for etiquette consultants.

Corporations

The business world offers many opportunities for etiquette consultants. As discussed earlier in this guide, you can use your skills to train supervisors, new hires, and other employees. You can train staff on general business etiquette, or offer programs on a variety of specific etiquette issues, such as email etiquette, telephone etiquette, or even holiday party etiquette.

The corporations you decide to target will likely depend on your networking contacts and personal background and preferences. For example, if your background is in the financial industry, then you may want to market your services to financial companies because you understand their needs and have contacts in the industry.

Other companies that can benefit from etiquette training include companies in the hospitality industry, health care providers, call centers, and any company doing business overseas. However, etiquette training – particularly for customer service and sales personnel – is needed in virtually all industries, so you can certainly target any companies you feel could benefit from your services.

To find companies to contact you can use your local telephone directory or an industry directory. Many Chambers of Commerce put out an annual member book that includes contact names and numbers for local companies.

Using a directory, combined with information from company websites, you can compile a list containing information such as:

- Company name
- Business phone number
- Decision-makers' names and contact information
- Size and location of company
- Key facts about the company and industry

TIP: Note the name of the company owner, President, or CEO. Even if you won't be contacting them directly, at some point you may be meeting with them.

If you don't have personal contacts, you can approach companies directly. While the human resources department often hires trainers, it is a good idea to also approach decision-makers in all of the appropriate departments you want to work with. For example, if you offer telephone etiquette, you can contact the call center manager. If you offer business and dining etiquette programs for salespeople, you can contact the vice president of sales, sales directors, and sales managers throughout the organization. Contacting as many decision-makers as possible within an organization can improve your odds of getting hired more quickly.

Realize that it may take months to break into a particular organization. Even though the sales manager wants you to present a series of seminars to the sales staff, it can take time to set a date, get budget approval, and get a contract signed. However, once you are chosen to do one presentation for a corporation, there will probably be opportunities for future programs within the same company.

Professional and Trade Associations

There are professional associations of doctors, lawyers, managers, administrative assistants, public relations professionals, and many other occupations. Likewise, there are trade associations for people who work in particular industries, such as banking, fashion, travel, insurance, and many others.

Among the thousands of associations are local, state and provincial, national and international groups. Many of these groups hold an annual convention (which may be called an "annual meeting" or conference"), and a variety of other events for their members, ranging from awards banquets to seminars, any of which may require speakers. Etiquette topics such as those you offer to local service clubs are also popular with associations.

Look for local associations through your telephone directory or networking contacts. For ideas of groups to contact you can check the following sites which have links to numerous associations: the first is the *American Society of Association Executives: Search Page*. They are located at **www.asaenet.org/directories/associationsearch.cfm**. The second is *CharityVillage Directory of Professional Associations*, which you can find at **www.charityvillage.com/cv/nonpr/profas.asp**.

Other Organizations

Virtually any organization that prepares people for the business world can use the services of a skilled etiquette consultant to offer training programs. When you are networking you will meet people involved with a variety of organizations. Learn more about what they do and ask yourself how you could help them.

Here are a few examples of organizations to consider, and the ways that an etiquette consultant can assist them.

Professional Recruiting Firms

These companies groom clients for new careers or new jobs. Along with how to write a resume and how to ace an interview, business etiquette skills are definitely something many new clients need.

In the U.S., you can find the *U.S. Employment Agency Index* at **www.employmentagencies.ca/USA/index.htm**. In Canada, look for the Directory of Canadian Recruiters at the following address: **www.directoryofrecruiters.com/wwwsites.html**. Similar directories exist for other countries.

Colleges

Institutions of higher education want to turn out the best and most well prepared students possible, and that is the basis that you will use to get your foot in the door. Soon-to-be graduates are often nervous about their skills and are looking for ways to make the transition from campus to the workplace. A workshop on interview etiquette or workplace etiquette may be very well received.

You can search for colleges and universities at *Peterson's Education Portal*, located at **www.petersons.com**. For Canadian Universities and Colleges, go to *SchoolFinder* at **www.schoolfinder.com**.

Economic Development Organizations

Another area where your services may be needed is with the local, state, or provincial business development organization. These organizations have representatives who meet with business representatives from around the world to try to convince them to do business in their community. Your workshops on business etiquette and international protocol could help them make a good impression on the businesses they're courting.

As mentioned in section 2.4.1, the organization that handles business development varies. It may be handled by an economic development department at the local, state or provincial level, or it may be done by the chamber of commerce, the Mayor's office, the tourism board, a visitor center, or the convention and visitor's bureau. Contact one or more of your local organizations to find out who handles the economic development role in your community.

5.4.2 Your First Meeting

Getting a Meeting Set Up

Once you have your client wish list, you have to figure out how to reach the decision-making person and get an appointment with them. This may be as easy as calling the office and asking the person who answers the phone how you get an appointment with Mr. Big, and getting an appointment for the next week. However, it may not be quite as easy. Executives with large organizations have people in place so that they don't have to field every call or email.

Sample Phone Script

You:	Hello, Ms. Decision Maker, and thank you so much for taking the time to talk with me.
Decision Maker:	My assistant told me that you have some training that I might be interested in for my employees.
You:	I was telling him about my Effective Email training class. It's a short workshop on the etiquette of email—how to politely address clients, when to copy others into the conversation, and what type of email is inappropriate in a company setting. I present it in a way that is fun and engaging, but also gets a strong message across.
Decision Maker:	You know he's right, email is out of hand around here. I might just be interested in that.
You:	I also have several other workshops geared towards communication etiquette in the workplace. Can we set up a meeting to discuss what workshop might be best for your people?
Decision Maker:	Sure, let me put you over to my assistant and he'll put you on my calendar.

If you have trouble getting through, something as simple as a genuinely nice attitude can help you get through to the big boss. You can also try calling just after 5:00 p.m. or before 8:00 a.m. Many busy executives get to their offices early in the morning and stay long after everyone has left. If you must leave a voicemail message, leave it after hours. It's the first message they will hear the next morning.

> **TIP:** Don't get frustrated and fire off a quick and easy email about the benefits of your business to the decision-maker. This is too easy to delete with the click of a button.

Once you get the decision-maker on the phone, it's time to sell your services. After a brief introduction of you and what you do, you can ask if the company has workshops, seminars or similar services for the employees or executives. This is a natural lead in to what you want to do. You can also ask if they ever used an etiquette consultant's services, and what the outcome was.

"No doesn't always mean no," says Jodi R.R. Smith of Mannersmith Etiquette Consulting in Boston. "It usually means no, not right now. I have had clients tell me no only to say yes when I called six months or even six years later."

Preparing to Meet

As etiquette consultants know, you only get one chance to make a first impression. You are the expert in etiquette, so look the part and act the part. This doesn't mean you have to be stuffy or rigid, but you need to be poised.

Always err on the side of caution when it comes to dressing for an meeting. You don't have to wear a three-piece suit, but you can dress professionally. Remember, you are the etiquette expert. The hiring manager will expect you to serve as a role model in all things etiquette, and that includes your appearance. Here are a couple of specific pointers:

- Skimp on jewelry. You don't want to jingle-jangle through your meeting. Women should go with something simple and understated. Men can just skip it all together, other than a wedding band or other significant ring.

- Stay away from loud colors and wild patterns. You want to be remembered for what you said, not your polka dot tie or zebra-printed scarf. Women should also apply makeup with a light hand.

Once someone agrees to meet with you, you'll need to prepare for the meeting. If you are feeling nervous, realize that the fact that a busy person has agreed to meet with you means they are interested in your services. While there is no guarantee that you will get a particular client, if someone has a need for your services and is meeting with you, you have a good chance of getting their business.

Your purpose during this meeting is to turn a prospective client into a client. The way to do this is by identifying what your client needs and wants, so you can communicate how your services will benefit them.

This is where your interpersonal communication skills will really pay off (see section 2.2.2 if this is an area you need to improve). You can begin by giving a quick overview of your services, however, during your meeting you should mostly ask and listen. Aim to have your client do about 80% of the talking. (Of course take your cue from the client. If they prefer not to do a lot of talking, don't try to force it.)

Instead of describing all your services, focus specifically on what the client wants and explain how etiquette training can benefit the company and the employees. Before the meeting you should do some online research to learn about the industry and gather as much information on the company as you can (most companies have a tremendous amount of information on their websites).

Based on what the client says they need, you can present several different ideas for training or one-on-one coaching. Here are some good general topics to choose from and you will likely have many other ideas after reading this guide.

- Business etiquette overview
- Dining etiquette
- Telephone skills and cell phone etiquette
- Social etiquette

- The art of the introduction
- The etiquette "advantage" (etiquette for sales people)
- Networking etiquette
- International protocol
- Business meeting etiquette
- Trade show etiquette
- Company party etiquette

How you communicate with the client can be just as important as what you communicate. Many people have preconceived notions that etiquette will be a dry subject. By being enthusiastic during the meeting, you can show the decision maker that you will be able to get through to the participants in the training.

One manager we spoke with said he looks for "enthusiasm and outgoing personality" when hiring trainers for his company. Another mentioned the ability "to make training fun." Here are a few more of the qualities that hiring executives look for in an etiquette consultant:

- Solid knowledge of etiquette
- Confidence, and the ability to inspire it in others
- Friendliness
- Strong communication skills
- Motivation
- A team player

5.4.3 Creating a Winning Proposal

After meeting with the decision maker, he or she may be interested in seeing a written proposal. A proposal is a written document, usually in the form of a letter, outlining what you propose to do for an organization.

If you have done an effective job of identifying the client's needs during the meeting, the proposal should simply put in writing what you agreed to during the meeting. However, you may occasionally be asked to prepare a proposal when a client is not seriously interested in doing business with you. So before you invest hours in preparing the proposal consider whether or not it is a good investment of your time.

Why Organizations Ask for Proposals

Sometimes the request for a proposal may come "out of the blue" from an employer you haven't approached. The beginning consultant typically thinks this is great news. After all, why would they ask for a proposal if they were not interested? Actually, there are a number of reasons employers ask for proposals:

It May Be Necessary for the Job

In some cases, a proposal is necessary for the job. For example, many government departments require the decision-maker to review written proposals from several different prospects before a contract is awarded. They will often have formal RFP (request for proposal) guidelines for you to follow.

Likewise, if you have an idea for a continuing education course you would like to teach, most continuing education organizations will ask for a written proposal. The person you speak with should be able to tell you what they need in your proposal to make their decision.

If you pay attention to how they communicate with you, you should get a sense of how your proposal will be treated when it is received. Are they encouraging? Do they return your calls promptly? Do they sound positive about your chances? If the answer is "yes" and you want the job, it is probably worth your time to write the proposal. However, there may be times that writing a proposal will be a waste of your time and energy.

It May Be a "Brush Off"

Some employers find it difficult to say "no" and want to avoid a confrontation. They can delay saying no by having you submit a proposal. The employer can then say it is "under review" until you either give up or they finally work up the courage to tell you they are not interested.

It May Be Used to Confirm a Hiring Decision

The most common reason some employers ask for proposals is because they want to have written comparisons of several trainers. Often, they have a "preferred" trainer in mind, and the purpose of the written proposals is to help them confirm their decision, or show their supervisor or a hiring committee that they have "shopped around."

> **TIP:** If you are the preferred trainer you will know it. The employer will have discussed the program with you in detail, and you will have reached a tentative agreement to do the work. They will explain that their regulations require them to review written proposals and may even assure you that it will be "just a formality."

If you are the preferred trainer and you want the job, then it is worth your time to put together a proposal confirming the details you have discussed with the employer. Otherwise, your time might be better spent focusing on employers who are seriously interested in you.

What to Include in Your Proposal

If the company has a formal request for proposal process, you will use that as the guideline in preparing your proposal. A typical RFP is a document that provides information about the organization, their training needs, the target audience, what they require in a proposal, and instructions for submission of the proposal. Here is an example of the type of information expected in a proposal:

- A description of your company
- Demonstration of your ability to develop and deliver the program
- Detailed description of the approach you will take in the training
- A proposed timetable
- A fixed price quote for development and delivery of the program
- Specific resources (such as trainers who work for you) that you will assign to the project
- References from organizations you've done similar programs for

Once you have all the elements of the proposal together, you can place them in a heavy portfolio, which you can find at any office supply store. Here is a detailed look at key elements that can make up your proposal:

Company Overview or Bio

The first thing in your proposal will be a brief summary of who you are and what services you offer. It can be one sentence or half a page long, but don't run much beyond the half of a page. People don't want to read about your early trials or your childhood days on a farm, they are only interested in how your background makes you a better etiquette consultant.

Sample Bio

Elaine Brocher spent ten years working in the human resources field, where she worked one-on-one with people and taught a variety of different skills. She conducted workshops on many different topics, but her favorites were always the ones on how to act and how to treat people.

Elaine became the company expert on etiquette, which was no small feat, because the company spanned the globe and employed thousands of people from many different nationalities. In her years as the etiquette expert Elaine learned the finer points of business etiquette, both in North America and abroad. She became the in-house expert on international protocol and flew around the world training executives. Also, Elaine coordinated in-house training on communication etiquette, email etiquette, telephone etiquette, customer care, and client relationships.

After five years as the company etiquette expert, Elaine set out on her own. For more than ten years now Elaine has taught etiquette to different people in different industries all across the state. She is an expert on all things etiquette, and has great insight into how etiquette can impact client and employee relations. Elaine also has her years of training in international protocol, which is priceless to those companies who are looking to do business on an international scale.

Services Offered

How this section of your proposal is laid out depends on your client's wants. You will include the specific services they want you to perform and any samples of handouts and even a workshop itinerary. If you are creating customized materials, then it's a good idea to create one small part just to show how your work will combine the corporate information with your etiquette information (see sample below). Once you land the contract, you'll have a jump start.

Sample Workshop Outline

Mind Your Phone Manners

This workshop focuses on the basics of telephone and cellular phone etiquette. Covered in the workshop are:

- Creating appropriate outgoing messages for your phone
- Leaving an effective message
- Returning calls: when, how, and why not
- When NOT to be available – cellular phone tips
- When someone else answers your phone
- Call Waiting and Caller I.D. – how to use these tools
- Special speaker phone rules

The workshop is interactive and I will use role-plays along with PowerPoint to present the material in a fun and informative way. The workshop includes the following handouts:

- Sample message scripts
- Dos and Don'ts of cellular phones
- Six Simple Cell Phone Rules

Duration: 2 hours

Price

This is your fee structure and how much you are being paid for each service you are providing. See section 4.2.4 on setting your fees. If you were presenting five half-day sessions at a rate of $1,000 per session, you could write it in your proposal as follows:

> The per session fee (for groups of up to 10 participants) is $1,000.00, for a total of $5,000.00 plus tax. For more than 10, add $50.00 per person per session plus tax.

References and Testimonials

These are references the company can contact to follow up on this information. So how do you get these? Say you've just completed a workshop on telephone etiquette for the Lions Club and the club president tells you that you've done a wonderful job. Ask him if you can use his words in your next brochure or proposal.

If he says yes, and most likely he will, just jot down what he just told you and offer to send it to him for his review. If you leave it up to him to write, he may forget or he may get too busy.

Send him the information the next day and follow up in a few days to make sure he's received it. Once he okays the information, put it in your materials. Here are a few samples for you to look at.

> "Mary Manners offers an incredible service. Her workshop on communication etiquette gave my staff some much needed skills. They learned how to talk to each other more effectively and how to use email more appropriately. Finally, I stopped getting all those jokes forwarded. Thank you, Mary!"
>
> — Steven Cobb, XYZ Industries

> "Mary did a workshop for us on cellular rules, and she's great. Her information is on target and she gets right to it. She's a great speaker and the material she created for us was great. My employees now understand that talking on the phone at work is not only against the rules, it's rude."
>
> — Kevin Register, Amazing A's Restaurant

> "We had Mary in to teach our kids the basic of table etiquette. The kids loved her fun attitude, and you should see how great they all act at lunch now. Not perfect, but much, much better. At least now we hear a few pleases and thank yous."
>
> — Erika Phillips, Northern Elementary School

Proposal Resources

A number of companies specialize in writing proposals. You can find them by doing a web search for "writing proposals" and "contract." An excellent resource is Deborah Kluge's webpage with links on proposal writing and government contracting. You can find the site at **www.proposalwriter.com/links.html**. Another great resource is the book *Proven Proposal Strategies to Win More Business*, by Herman Holtz.

6. Success Stories

You have nearly reached the end of the *FabJob Guide to Become an Etiquette Consultant* and are closer to achieving your dream. To further inspire and inform you, the guide concludes with a number of profiles of professionals who have been successful in the etiquette field.

6.1 Meet Mary Mitchell

Mary Mitchell
www.themitchell.org

Mary Mitchell remembers her terror. She didn't know anybody and didn't speak the language, yet there she was, in a Middle Eastern country where what she did could make or break her husband's success as an

s very real fear," she now recalls. "I didn't
behave, but I did know that my husband's
d on my ability to be socially acceptable."

and Mitchell became accomplished as
ed, the corporate wife," meanwhile pur-
eting consultant to corporate clients. "I
oyed," she explains. "My father was a doc-
used to hearing the word 'job'." Even so, corporate
client service can be a challenge, and, she adds, "I kept getting fired from marketing."

Things blossomed when corporate executives started telling Mitchell that their employees "weren't able to advance a business agenda in a social setting." Knowing firsthand what it was like to be intimidated by the social demands of corporate culture, she established The Mitchell Organization in Philadelphia in 1989, and launched what would become her career as consultant, author, and corporate trainer with special expertise in etiquette.

In the early days, Mitchell did a lot of consulting for free and advises others never to reject programs that don't pay. "You'll always get something in return." Free lectures and a no-fee column for the *Great Valley Business News* in Philadelphia helped bring business in and led to a nationally syndicated etiquette column and the first of Mitchell's five books.

To hone her skills, Mitchell read everything written by Letitia Baldrige, America's reigning etiquette doyenne. "She had been in the same situation I had," Mitchell says, "and had extensive international experience. Eventually we met, and she's been my mentor ever since." Letitia Baldrige wrote the foreword to Mitchell's most recent book: *Class Acts: How Good Manners Create Good Relationships and Good Relationships Create Good Business*.

Today, Mitchell bills corporate clients for high-end management consulting, conducting workshops, seminars, lectures, and one-on-one sessions in the art of being an effective business communicator in social settings. She works with clients for anywhere from one hour to one year, depending on their needs, most of which involve fear. "There's a tremendous unspoken prejudice against people who don't know how to handle themselves," she explains, "particularly at tables. People are afraid of not getting a job or a client, and nobody tells you that you didn't get what you wanted because your manners were terrible."

The two biggest areas that hang business professionals up, Mitchell believes, are meetings and greetings. Technically gifted executives are often insecure or ignorant about how best to present themselves, how to make social introductions, how to walk into a room full of professional people. Such problems get bigger when people of different cultures encounter one another. "International customs are a big area," she says.

Another big area is appropriate dress. Mitchell cites a program she conducted for fast-track business students: "Here were the University of Pennsylvania's best and brightest assembled at a fancy restaurant for a dining tutorial, and two guys walked in with shirtsleeves and no jackets. 'Guys,' I said, "think about how you're being perceived.'"

Mitchell emphasizes the benefit of keeping her own skills up to date. "I could probably write another book," she quips, "about some of the gaffes I've made and survived." And she continues to do pro bono work with children: "I go into grade schools in challenged neighborhoods in Philadelphia. I teach them how to disagree without being disagreeable, how to criticize and take criticism without becoming defensive."

Some client challenges are unexpected. Mitchell describes a project for the U.S. Navy, helping military personnel translate "Navyspeak" into "corporatespeak" for private-sector contractors. "In finalizing the assignment via email," she says, "my contact closed with his name, followed by 'XO,' which in the Navy means executive officer. I emailed him back: 'You need this workshop more than you think. In my world you've just sent me a kiss and a hug.'"

Mitchell has done relatively little formal marketing because her word of mouth promotion has been so strong. She does, however, have an Internet presence explaining her company's services and featuring her books, and she does a lot of TV.

She's also confident about her company's future. "My professional mission is to take the starch out of a subject that people think is stuffy," she says. "Etiquette is a way of helping people be effective in [communicating] the message they want to get across."

6.2 Meet Colleen A. Rickenbacher

Colleen Rickenbacher, Inc.
www.colleenrickenbacher.com

Colleen A. Rickenbacher has had a successful career as an etiquette specialist for more than nine years, with clients ranging from Anthem Blue Cross Blue Shield, Federal Express, and the International Association of Fire Chiefs, to GlaxoSmithKline, Four Seasons Resorts and the National Speakers Association. She is the author of the book *Be on Your Best Business Behavior*, a resource to help businesspeople polish their etiquette skills and give well-mannered attention to their clients.

Rickenbacher has an impressive resume in the field of protocol etiquette, but it was never her plan to become a specialist. Witnessing some major social faux pas at a company dinner some 12 years ago changed the course of Rickenbacher's career, which at that time was with the Dallas Convention and Visitors' Bureau as an event planner. During dinner, Rickenbacher noticed what she describes as a vast array of inappropriate behavior, from people ordering excessive amounts of expensive appetizers, dinners and drinks, to requesting doggie bags on their departure.

Rickenbacher, a longtime employee, later casually commented on the behavior to management in the company. "I suggested to our human resources head that we get someone in to do some dining etiquette protocol. He suggested I do it, and that is how the whole thing started," she recalled.

Rickenbacher gave herself a crash course in etiquette. "I bought all kinds of books and did the research [to do the class]," she said. "The chamber of commerce was in the same building and they heard I had given the presentation and asked me to do it for the chamber." For Rickenbacher, that was the start of a new career, which has since flourished.

An event planner for many years, Rickenbacher had 30 years experience in hospitality service. She received a Certified Meeting Professional

(CMP) designation in 1992 and later earned her Certified Special Events Professional (CMEP). With excellent observational, organizational, and communication skills, she made a smooth transition to becoming a speaker, a key role in her work in the field of etiquette protocol.

Her topics of presentations have included the proper etiquette concerning email, telephones, fax machines, and cell phones; as well as office protocol and dining etiquette.

There are a number of ways to become an etiquette specialist, according to Rickenbacher, and taking the route she did is one such way. There are many books, newspaper and magazine articles and columns on the topic, she says. There are also two organizations that provide many resources, the National Speakers Association and a new organization, the International Association of Protocol Consultants. Both associations have conferences with relevant speakers and offer other benefits to their members.

Once you have the background necessary, the next step is marketing. There are a number of ways to market yourself, according to Rickenbacher. One of the least expensive ways is to put together a website. “You don’t have to make it high-end or expensive,” she said. “But make sure you update it every six months.” As well as explaining what services you offer and your credentials, you should list your clients and any awards or recognition you receive.

Another simple but effective marketing tool is a business card. Make sure that it states that you are a speaker, Rickenbacher says.

Rickenbacher also suggests making a good quality video and using 60 seconds of the tape on your website. It is important that the video be of professional quality, she says, so be ready to spend some money on this commercial investment.

One of the biggest pitfalls newcomers to the field should avoid, Rickenbacher says, is doing all your first presentations for free. “I recommend that you get an honorarium, like a restaurant gift certificate, a day of golf, a day at the spa or free airfare, or you get paid as little as $25 to $50, because once you have done it for free it is hard to get something out of it later.”

Once you get a following, Rickenbacher suggests doing one low-cost presentation every three months. "That way you will get yourself out there, but they will have to fit their schedule around yours, instead of you fitting your schedule around them," she says.

Joining a group of speakers who all specialize in different niches is also a way to help promote yourself and network among your peers. It also may help you find a mentor, even if it is someone who is not in your specific field. "They can still help you out if you have some questions about getting started or doing presentations," she says. "That in itself is worth a million dollars."

6.3 Meet Jacqueline Whitmore

Jacqueline Whitmore
www.etiquetteexpert.com

Miss Manners beware: Jacqueline Whitmore is becoming one of the top names in the etiquette industry. She has appeared on CNN, the Travel Channel, FOX and CNNRadio, and has been profiled in some of the country's top publications: *USA Today*, *The New York Times, Glamour, Woman's World, Men's Health*, and *The Wall Street Journal*. She is also the author of Business Class: Etiquette Essentials for Success at Work, the publisher of the monthly etiquette e-newsletter The Protocol Post, and the holiday etiquette expert for Office Depot.

Whitmore, a former flight attendant and entertainer at Sea World of Florida, became the founder and director of The Protocol School of Palm Beach, which specializes in business etiquette and professional enhancement seminars. Whitmore is also the cell phone etiquette spokesperson for the Sprint phone company, for which she makes radio and television appearances. So how did she do it?

Before starting her own company, Whitmore worked in public relations for a luxurious resort hotel. While working there, Whitmore attended the Protocol School of Washington, became certified in business etiquette, and was named the hotel's first protocol officer. "I had an interest in etiquette and protocol because I worked in the hospitality industry for more than 12 years," she says. "For me it was a nice fit with the educational background that I had already attained."

Whitmore has worked in a variety of industries. She has been an international flight attendant; a singer, dancer, and actor at Sea World of Florida; and a special events coordinator with the Walt Disney World Dolphin Hotel, among others.

Although Whitmore's background in public relations and hospitality helped her in her work as an etiquette consultant, she believes there is not one type of background needed for this field. Putting your background to use, whether it is in hospitality or at a car dealership, is one way to find your business niche, which Whitmore suggests for those new to the field. "When you focus on more than one [niche market] you tend to spread yourself too thin," she says.

Once you find your niche, the next step is marketing. "I would say advertising is not as effective as writing news releases and getting out and just speaking," she says. "Speak for free at chamber of commerce luncheons, rotary clubs, and women's groups. That is the best way to get out there."

Getting your foot in the door is easier than you think. Call local groups and associations and offer your services. "Tell them, 'I am an expert in executive etiquette and I can speak to your members about how to network more effectively, or how to remember names or make a better impression at their next holiday party.' You offer your services free of charge and they generally will ask you to come in and speak for 20 minutes," she says. "It is your way of getting your face in front of a lot of people, a lot of decision-makers who could potentially hire you."

Making the step from non-paying clients to paid work may take some time, and you must have patience and perseverance. "You have to give before you get," Whitmore explains. "You have to get yourself in front of people who can potentially pay you for your services. It is better than calling somebody cold and saying, 'Hello my name is...' They are going to hang up on you. But when you go to where they are and you are a speaker endorsed by the chamber, it gives you that added credibility."

There are some misperceptions people have about working as an etiquette consultant, according to Whitmore. “People think they are going have any business for three or four months, but you should utilize that time with something productive like marketing, that you wouldn’t have time to do if you were on the road speaking.”

Internet marketing is one such area. “You can work on a website and link yourself with search engines,” Whitmore says. Writing articles on etiquette can also help you get your foot in the door. You have to be creative and a little aggressive to be published in magazines or you local newspaper. “Submit articles, give them ideas, give them samples of what you have done, do the thinking for them,” she says. “It is like fishing, sometimes you won’t catch anything, sometimes you will catch something big and sometimes you will catch something small.”

You can also write press releases about your business and the services you offer, or any award you have received, Whitmore says. Most local newspapers have a business section with a column where these types of achievements are noted. “If you get some sort of promotion or receive some honor, submit that,” she says. “It may be just one sentence that gets in the paper, but you would be surprised how many people read that.”

“Whenever you pursue a career in etiquette and protocol there will be many highlights,” summarizes Whitmore. “You have the opportunity to meet a diverse group of people all over the country. It will take you to places that perhaps you have never been before.”

7. Resources

There are hundreds of etiquette books covering all aspects of etiquette. To help you add to the titles you refer to as an etiquette consultant, here are a selection of titles to get you started. You can find many others at **www.amazon.com**.

General Etiquette Books

- The Amy Vanderbilt Complete Book of Etiquette: 50th Anniversary Edition, *by Nancy Tuckerman and Nancy Dunnan*

- *Letitia Baldridge's New Manners for New Times: A Complete Guide to Etiquette*, by Letitia Baldridge

- *Emily Post's Etiquette, 17th Edition*, by Peggy Post

- *Miss Manners' Basic Training: The Right Thing to Say*, by Judith Martin

Business Etiquette Books

- *Be on Your Best Business Behavior: How to Avoid Social and Professional Faux Pas*, by Colleen A. Rickenbacher
- *Business Class: Etiquette Essentials for Success at Work*, by Jacqueline Whitmore
- *Business Etiquette for Dummies*, by Sue Fox
- *Class Acts: How Good Manners Create Good Relationships and Good Relationships Create Good Business*, by Mary Mitchell
- *The Complete Idiot's Guide to Business Etiquette*, by Mary Mitchell with John Corr
- *Do's and Taboos Around the World for Women in Business*, by Roger Axtell
- *The Etiquette Advantage in Business: Personal Skills for Professional Success*, by Peggy Post
- *1-800-Courtesy: Connecting With a Winning Telephone Image*, by Terry Wildemann
- *The Official Book of Electronic Etiquette*, by Charles Winters and Anne Winters

International Protocol Books

Author Ann Marie Sabath has a series of books (the International Business Etiquette series) on etiquette in Europe, Asia and the Pacific Rim, and Latin America. Another series by Mary Murray Bosrock called Put Your Best Foot Forward looks at doing business in all of these regions, as well as Russia and Mexico.

- *International Business Etiquette: Europe*, by Ann Marie Sabath
- *International Business Etiquette: Asia and the Pacific Rim*, by Ann Marie Sabath

- *International Business Etiquette: Latin America*, by Ann Marie Sabath
- *Put Your Best Foot Forward: Europe*, by Mary Murray Bosrock
- *Put Your Best Foot Forward: South America*, by Mary Murray Bosrock
- *Put Your Best Foot Forward: Asia*, by Mary Murray Bosrock
- *Put Your Best Foot Forward: Russia*, by Mary Murray Bosrock
- *Put Your Best Foot Forward: Mexico and Canada*, by Mary Murray Bosrock
- *Kiss, Bow, or Shake Hands: How to Do Business in Sixty Countries*, by Terri Morrison, Wayne A. Conaway, and George A. Borden
- *Diplomatic Handbook*, by Ralph Feltham

Dining Etiquette Books

- *Elements of Etiquette: A Guide to Table Manners in an Imperfect World*, by Craig Claiborne
- *Miss Manners' Basic Training: Eating*, by Judith Martin
- *In the Royal Manner: Expert Advice on Etiquette and Entertaining from the Former Butler to Diana, Princess of Wales*, by Paul Burrell
- *The Rituals of Dinner: The Origins, Evolution, Eccentricities, and Meaning of Table Manners*, by Margaret Visser

Children's Etiquette

- *365 Manners Kids Should Know: Games, Activities, and Other Fun Ways to Help Children Learn Etiquette*, by Sheryl Eberly
- *How Rude! Teenager's Guide to Good Manners, Proper Behavior, and Not Grossing People Out*, by Alex Packer

Wedding Etiquette

- *Emily Post's Wedding Etiquette: Cherished Traditions and Contemporary Ideas for a Joyous Celebration (4th Edition)*, by Peggy Post

- *Emily Post's Wedding Planner*, by Peggy Post

Miscellaneous Books

- *Believers and Beliefs: A Practical Guide to Religious Etiquette for Business and Social Occasions*, by Gayle Coluitt White

- *The Art and Etiquette of Gift Giving*, by Dawn Bryant

- *Raving Fans: A Revolutionary Approach to Customer Service*, by Ken Blanchard and Sheldon Bowles

- *Writing Thank-You Notes: Finding The Perfect Words*, by Gabrielle Goodwin and David Macfarlane

More Fabulous Guides

Find out how to break into the "fab" job of your dreams with FabJob career guides. You can choose from more than 75 titles including:

Get Paid to Help People Look Fabulous

Imagine having an exciting high paying job showing people and companies how to make a fabulous impression. **FabJob Guide to Become an Image Consultant** shows you how to:

- Do image consultations and advise people about: total image makeovers, communication skills, wardrobe, and corporate image
- Start an image consulting business, price your services, and find clients
- Select strategic partners such as makeup artists, hair stylists, and cosmetic surgeons
- Have the polished look and personal style of a professional image consultant

Get Paid to Give Business Advice

Imagine having a prestigious career helping businesses and other organizations identify and resolve problems. The **FabJob Guide to Become a Business Consultant** shows you how to:

- Learn the stages involved in a consulting project and develop your consulting skills (no business degree is required)
- Get hired by a management consulting firm or become an internal consultant for a corporation
- Start your own consulting firm (plus how to be certified as a "professional" consultant)
- How to get clients for your business (includes a sample proposal and consulting agreement)

Visit www.FabJob.com to order guides today!

More Fabulous Guides

Find out how to break into the "fab" job of your dreams with FabJob career guides. You can choose from more than 75 titles including:

Get Paid to Help People Achieve Success

Imagine having a fulfilling career coaching people how to achieve success in their careers, relationships, and life. In the **FabJob Guide to Become a Life Coach** you will learn:

- How to choose a coaching specialization such as corporate and executive coaching, relationship coaching, or spiritual coaching
- How to help clients identify problems and set goals (includes a sample coaching session, questions to ask clients, and sample coaching exercises to use with individuals and groups)
- How to start and run a part-time or full-time coaching business and get clients (includes a sample client intake form and client contracts)

Get Paid to Plan Events

Imagine getting paid to use your planning skills to organize a variety of events including corporate meetings, conferences and large public events. **FabJob Guide to Become an Event Planner** shows you how to:

- Teach yourself event planning (includes step-by-step advice for planning an event)
- Make your event a success and avoid disasters
- Get a job as an event planner with a corporation, convention center, country club, tourist attraction, resort or other event industry employer
- Start your own event planning business, price your services, and find clients
- Be certified as a professional event planner

Visit www.FabJob.com to order guides today!

Get paid to plan weddings!
FabJob Guide to
Become a Wedding Planner
Includes CD-ROM!
Catherine Goulet and Jan Riddell
Third Edition

Get paid to speak!
FabJob Guide to
Become a Motivational Speaker
Includes CD-ROM!
Tag Goulet

Get paid to decorate!
FabJob Guide to
Become an Interior Decorator
Includes CD-ROM!
Tag Goulet and Catherine Goulet